GOD'S
FIRST
WORDS

GOD'S FIRST WORDS

STUDIES IN GENESIS
HISTORIC, PROPHETIC AND
EXPERIMENTAL

By G. D. Watson

Shoals, Indiana

God's First Words

PUBLISHED BY KINGSLEY PRESS
PO Box 973
Shoals, IN 47581
USA
Tel. (800) 971-7985
www.kingsleypress.com
E-mail: sales@kingsleypress.com

ISBN: 978-1-937428-14-3

First Kingsley Press edition 2012

Printed in the United States of America

Contents

1

God's First Words

Have you ever thought of the first word that God ever spoke in the vastness of eternity? It has been revealed to us in Scripture, namely, "In the beginning was the Word," and also "In the beginning God." The first word that the infinite God ever spoke constituted the expression of His eternal Son, the "logos," Who existed from eternity in the bosom of the Father.

It is of necessity that God should know Himself, and this knowledge which God has of Himself forms the personality of the eternal Son, for God must know Himself from eternity; and hence the person of the only begotten Son must of necessity be as eternal as the Father Himself. When the Father spoke His first word, that was the expression of the person of the Son of God, and all other words that God has ever spoken are through His eternal Son and because of His Son and for His Son. In the true sense, when any one speaks a word, it must be the expression of one's nature, the articulation of the inward character which the speaker has.

The old theologians tell us that of necessity God spoke one word and that word was His Son, and that Satan tried to counterfeit God and he thought that he would imitate God in speaking a word, but when he uttered his word it was a lie. This corresponds with the words of Jesus, that the Devil is a liar and the father of it; so that every lie in the universe has been propagated from that first lie of which the Devil is the father. Just as truly as God spoke His first word, which was infinite truth, and all the truth in the universe proceeds from the truth of that primeval utterance, so every lie in the universe proceeds from that first lie which the Devil spoke. In the deepest and truest sense, nobody can speak a word contrary to the real inwardness of his nature. The word must always precede the act in the order of nature.

The creation is a product of God's word, for He made all things and upholds all things by the word of His power. When Solomon offered that wonderful prayer at the dedication of the temple, he said that what God had promised with His mouth He had fulfilled or accomplished with His hand (2 Chron. 6:15).

Moses was commanded to put on the hem of the garment of the High Priest a bell and a pomegranate round about the garment, but the bell came first and the pomegranate came next. The bell signifies testimony, speech, prophecy, and the pomegranate signifies fruit or action. Thus we see the word came first and the fruit came next.

Jesus preached His first sermon in Nazareth, after receiving the Holy Ghost; and after that He wrought His first miracle of turning water into wine. But the sermon came first and the miracle came after.

God's Word flows out from His very nature and is the expression of the fulness of His character. The book of Genesis contains God's first words in His revelation to the human race, and these first words are the pattern and sample of all other words in the Bible. I discovered some years ago that every doctrine that is taught in the Scripture is first mentioned or referred to in the book of Genesis, and that this wonderful book is the seed bed of every growth in the entire scope of divine revelation.

As we go through the Bible we find that the first words contained in Genesis are enlarged and unfolded in a great many different directions and applications, but the words themselves are never changed and they are never any more perfect in the last book in the Bible than they are in the first. God's words never need any correction or any improvement, but only to be unfolded and applied as time and generations go by.

It is a necessity in the creation that the verb must always flow out of the noun, which is simply saying that every act of every creature in the whole world must correspond with the name, that is, with the nature of that creature. We say the sun shines, the wind blows, the bird sings, and so on through all the ranks of created beings. But the light flows out from the nature of the sun, and the song from the nature of the bird, and the lie flows out from the nature of Satan, and so we say of God's love, for of necessity the love flows out from His name or His nature.

God cannot lie, because before He could tell a lie He must first cease to be God, and as long as He is the God that He has been from eternity, so long it will be impossible for Him to lie, because He must act out the contents of His character. That which is true of God is true also of all the creatures that He has made, for everything must express the contents of its nature.

This proves that no man can speak out from his heart the things of God in reality until he is born again and has the nature of God imparted to his heart, and then it is out of that new spiritual nature that he can speak and act the things of God. The apostle calls our sinful, fallen nature the old man, and that old man can never speak the things of God, but of necessity will speak the things that belong to the carnal mind. Hence we see the infinite necessity of the new birth.

The birth we have from Adam will of necessity express the things of Adam, and it is only when we are born from above, born of God, that we can speak and act the things of God. As God's first words revealed His inward character, so we cannot speak our first words in the Holy Ghost until we have an inward being produced by the Holy Ghost out of which we can speak and act the things of Christ.

I want us, in these chapters, to go through the book of Genesis and pick out God's first words on the various subjects which are mentioned in this beginning of all books and all revelation of God to man.

2

"In the Beginning God" (Gen. 1:1).

No other book in the universe could ever begin like this except it were the book of God. These first words in the Bible prove that the book has a divine Author—that it is not an invention of the human mind, for the very first expression is of such a character as to put it beyond all the thinking of the natural mind. There is no attempt to prove the existence of God. There is no prelude. But out from the vast eternity comes the simple, sublime expression that God was at the beginning, and He was before the beginning, because He was there in all His eternal perfections when the beginning started. The beginning did not make God, but God made the beginning, proving that He existed from eternity.

The word "God" is in the plural form and signifies unmistakably the plurality in the divine persons. The Hebrew word for God is "El." The plural form of that word is "Elohim," which is the term used in the first verse in the Bible. And then in the second verse there is made known the person of the eternal Spirit, for it says, "The Spirit of God moved," or more properly it should be "brooded on the face of the waters." So here we have at the beginning of the Bible the doctrine of the ever blessed Trinity, the three Divine Persons existing as one God, with one nature, one substance, one eternity, one glory, one character, and yet in three distinct personalities.

God is an infinite divine communion. The Father is supreme. The Son is generated from eternity in the bosom of the Father. The Holy Ghost proceeds eternally from the Father and the Son. There is only one Father, not two Fathers, Who is unbegotten, supreme in everything. There is only one Son, Who is generated or born eternally in the bosom of the Father. There is only one Holy Spirit, not born, not generated, but proceeding eternally from the Father through the Son. The Godhead is of one substance, but the three

Divine Persons are distinct in their mode of existence and in their expression and in their personal offices. Hence when God said, "Let us make man," there was a community of counsel and of authority and a perfect cooperation of all the Divine Persons.

It is impossible for any human mind to conceive of how God could exist from all eternity. In my younger years I have often tried to go back in imagination and attempt to grasp how the ever living God could exist from eternity without any beginning, but I never was able to apprehend an unbeginning existence such as God has. The Psalmist attempted to grasp the same thing, but he said it was too high for him, he could not attain unto it.

This proves that every created mind in the universe is in-finitely below God in capacity. All that any created intelligence can do is to lie at God's feet and look up in adoring wonder and forever and ever admire and worship that eternal, self-existent, all adorable God with absolute worship and trust and abandonment to Him without ever being able to fathom His infinite perfections, or to comprehend His unbeginning existence.

The very words, "In the beginning God," show that He must come first in all things in the universe, not only first in existence, but as His creatures it is His right to be first in all things to us, first in our worship, our obedience, our faith, our plans, our lives, first in all our difficulties, the first one to be consulted, the first one to be honored, the first one to be thanked, the first one to be recognized; that at all times and in all places and under all circumstances He should come first.

To worship God means a great deal more than prayer or service or good works or faith; it is to be delighted with Him, to enjoy Him, to find our supreme contentment in Him, and to feel in our hearts a sweet jealousy for His honor and for giving Him the first place in all things.

The first name by which God is called is used clear through the Bible. Often that name is unfolded into other names as we go through the Scriptures. The different names that are unfolded from His first name are according to the different stages in which He reveals Himself, and according to the different relationships which

He assumes toward the world and the human race. Just as the Son of God proceeds by an eternal generation from the bosom of the Father, so the other names of God proceed out from the bosom of that first name, Elohim.

The second name that God takes is that of Jehovah, found for the first time in Genesis 2:4. The name Jehovah reveals God in relation to His own people, and unfolds a more personal relationship between God and man. The root meaning of Elo-him is omnipotence, almighty power; but the root meaning of the name Jehovah is eternal, self-existent life, the One Who has always lived and will live forever, a fountain of self-existent life.

The third name that God reveals Himself by is that of Adon, found in Genesis 15:2. The root meaning of this word "Adon" is that of a pillar, a supporter, a sustainer, to bear up, to protect, to defend. This name belongs more especially to the Second Person in the Godhead, the Son of God, and is prophetic of His relation to mankind as an incarnate Saviour and Redeemer and Lord. This word "Adon" is also used in the Scriptures of human beings, but always in a lofty and honorable sense, as husband, lord, protector, as where Sarah calls Abraham "my lord;" the word is Adoni and not Jehovah. So this name first used in Genesis 15:2 indicates the relation of the Son of God as Redeemer and Supporter, a husband to His elect saints.

The fourth name that God reveals Himself by is that of El-Shaddai, and occurs for the first time in Genesis 17:1. The root of the word signifies an exhaustless fountain, an ever flowing supply, sufficient for every need. The word is sometimes used of a mother's breast which supplies nourishment for the infant. This word, in a special way, sets forth the eternal procession and outflow of the Holy Ghost from the heart of the eternal Father. The name indicates God outpouring Himself into His people and corresponds with the outpouring of the Holy Ghost upon believers. This name was used for the first time when God called Abraham to walk before Him and be perfect. God revealed to Abraham that, in spite of the wickedness of his own nature, the Almighty God could supply him with a stream of divine life and strength and grace sufficient to purify and make him to walk before God with perfect integrity and uprightness of heart, and possess an experience of pure love and charity by which he could please God.

As we study the successive giving of these names, we see how these first words in the names of God indicate the progress of God's revelation to mankind, and also the progress of relationships unfolded between God and man, and also the progressive steps in the life of faith and fellowship with God.

3

"God Created" (Gen. 1:1).

We have first the name of God and then the act of God. John tells us that the "Word was with God in the beginning, and the Word was God, and that all things which are created were created by that Word." We sometimes hear it said that God made the universe out of nothing, but we do not find any such expression in the Bible. On the other hand, the Scriptures teach us that the universe was formed by the word of God; God created all things out of His word. In other words, His words became solidified and the vast creation is the word of God made solid, firm, substantial. We read "He spake, and it was done; He commanded, and it stood fast;" and also we read that all things are upheld by the word of His power. We also read that He sent His word and healed them. The apostle tells us that the creation was not made out of preexisting materials or of things which do appear. As the eternal Son of God is the outspoken Word of the Father, so the creation of the universe is the active expression of the Son of God by the word of His power. We are told that the Father made nothing, but made all things by His Son; so that the Son of God stands in between the created universe and the person of the eternal Father. The Son of God is the connecting link between the Father and the universe. The creation is not God, but exists separate and apart from the person of God, because it is a product of His work and not an essential part of His being.

There has always been a class of thinkers that never could distinguish between the eternal existence of God and the created universe, and we call them Pantheists, because the word "pantheism" means that everything is a part of God. Mr. Emerson was the most celebrated writer in recent times of the school of pantheism, and he never seemed able, with all his brilliant intellect, to distinguish between a personal God and the works of that God. In other words, many seem unable to discern between evolution and creation. The Bible, from beginning to end, teaches creation as against evolution. There is an infinite gap between a thing being created and being evolved out of some previous substance. The question has often been propounded, Which existed first, the hen or the egg? Creation teaches that the hen existed first and she laid the egg, but evolution teaches that the egg existed first and evolved the hen. The difference between these two theories is absolutely infinite. God did not make the egg first, but made the hen first. Every word in the Bible respecting creation affirms that God made the tree first and the tree bore the fruit; that God made the animal first and the animal produced the off-spring; that God made the fishes first and the birds and every creature and that each creature, whether animate or inanimate, whether animal or vegetable, produced its species after its kind. Hence the whole teaching of evolution is absolutely atheistic and a denial of God and of creation and leads to every form of falsehood in doctrine, in life, in morals and everything else.

Now let us remember that while God created the universe and that its existence is not to be confounded with His own existence, yet Scripture teaches that God pervades all things and upholds all things by His presence and word and power. The Psalmist says, "If I make my bed in hell, God is there," but God is not hell. However, He pervades it with His presence; just as God is not the ocean, though He pervades every atom with His presence; and God is not a man, though He pervades every atom of our being with His presence. Electricity pervades every grain of sand on the earth and every drop of water, but electricity is a distinct thing from the sand and from the water.

God never created sin. He created an archangel named Lucifer, and that archangel made himself the Devil, and was the father of lies and the first sinner in the universe. God formed the constitution and faculties of Lucifer, but God did not form sin. Hence we must distinguish between God creating the universe and then between creatures forming a sinful character contrary to God and against His will and pleasure.

When man became a sinner, it required a plan of redemption to recreate in man a good, holy, spiritual life. It is just as impossible for a sinful soul to evolve a holy nature and life out of itself as it is for the dust to evolve out of itself a living man. No one can have the life of Christ in him except by a new creation, and the human heart can no more evolve out of its fallen nature a holy life than a drop of water or a grain of sand can evolve itself into an angel. The new birth and a clean heart must be by divine creation and not by evolution from the fallen Adam. Hence Scripture says, "Create in me a clean heart, O God; and renew a right spirit within me." The passage in 1 Peter which says, "Be ye holy," would be more literally expressed by the words "Be ye created holy," for the act of creation is involved in the original words. No man can make himself holy, and God does not require it; but God requires that we shall be willing for Him to recreate us in holiness and righteousness. We can be willing for Him to make us what we ought to be. Hence the creation of God not only applies to the primeval creation, but also to the new creation which is going forward under the redemption of Jesus Christ.

We shall see in succeeding chapters how the first creation is a model for the new creation, and how God is at the present time at work on the new creation under a plan of redemption.

4

The Old and New Creation

In the account that is given to us of the creation as described in the first chapter of Genesis, we have a perfect pattern of the new creation that is wrought out by the redemption of Jesus in the way in which God creates the soul anew in a spiritual life in Christ Jesus. It is not only God's first words in the old creation, but also His first words concerning the new birth and the formation of Christian character. Just as darkness was upon the face of the deep before the Creator began to form the world in its proper order, so there is darkness upon the soul of the natural man as he is born of Adam; and as it is said "the earth was without form and void," so in the spirit of the natural man as he exists in a fallen, sinful condition, everything in his whole inner being is without form and void and all the elements of his character are in a dark and confused state of existence. Let us notice the steps in the creation of the world and see how it agrees with the new life which a penitent believer receives by faith in Christ.

1. On the first day God said, "Let there be light." This was before the sun, moon and stars had been revealed in their distant forms, but there went forth through all the creation an all-pervading illumination dispelling the darkness. This is the first step that God takes in saving the soul; He sends forth the light of truth to put the sinner under conviction, and to enable him to discern that he is lost and needs a Saviour. Truth to the moral and spiritual nature is exactly what light is in the material world. It is only by the light of truth that a sinner can discern himself and see his sinful condition and see the need of a Saviour. We are told by St. John that Christ is the Light and that He gives light to every one that is born in the world; so that we are sure that every human soul that comes into this world has a measure of light imparted to it from the Lord Jesus Christ by virtue

of His incarnation and by virtue of His making atonement for all mankind. We are not able to know how much light is given to every human soul, only we are sure from the Word of God that no human being has ever existed that did not have light imparted to it from the Lord Jesus Christ in that measure which God sees is essential to meet the requirements of His plan and His will.

2. On the second day or period of creation God said, "Let there be a firmament in the midst of the waters, and let it divide the waters from above from those waters which are beneath." This firmament was a fixed division in the air, perhaps five or ten thousand feet above the earth, which separated the lower and heavier measure of air from the upper and thinner atmosphere in the upper regions of the sky. It is very evident from Scripture and the discovery of the laws of nature, that the greater part of the water that is now in the world was originally suspended in the upper regions of the air above this dividing line of the firmament, and that at the time of Noah's flood this firmament was made to break loose and the vast ocean of waters that were held in the form of vapor in the upper regions of the sky were let down upon the earth, causing the water on the earth in the present state of the world to form the greater part of the world's surface. This firmament was a dividing line, separating the water which was in the form of vapor from the lower water on the earth which existed in the form of liquid sea.

This is what takes place in the process of salvation in turning a sinner into a saint; that the Holy Ghost produces in the spirit of the penitent a dividing line between the soul and its sins and enables the seeking soul to see that its sins can be taken away, and that it is possible for Jesus, by His salvation, to produce a separation between the sinner and his sins. Sin is not an essential part of man's soul, for if that were so it would be impossible for God to save the sinner, but sin is a perversion of the dispositions of the heart and moral conception, and inward crookedness of desire and affection which can be separated from the soul, so that the human spirit can be made to exist as God originally intended it, and that the element of sin is a foreign character introduced by Satan and does not properly belong to the works of God. Thus we have here God's first words on a life of separation. Just as sin produces separation from God, so salvation through Jesus produces a separation from sin; and this is the office of the spiritual firmament which God produces in the new creation, corresponding to the firmament which He made to divide the waters on the second day of creation.

3. On the third day of creation God said, "Let the waters under the heaven," that is below the dividing line, "be gathered together in one place, and let the dry land appear." This shows us the third step in the process of salvation, namely, the gathering together of the elements of man's mental and moral nature into one form or one character in order that the true state of the soul may be made manifest. In man's evil and unsaved condition, all the elements of his character are scattered and confused, without harmony, without any proper government, without any distinct self-recognition of its true state. Under the law of conviction and the separating power of the Holy Ghost, there is a coming together of the various parts of man's mental and moral nature by which he is formed into a self-recognized, responsible subject of divine grace. We read that the prodigal son, in his terrible condition, feeding swine, when he got under true conviction it is said "he came to himself," a distinct recognition of what I am now talking about. Up to that time he did not have a proper recognition of himself, but under the light of divine conviction his scattered thoughts and feelings and convictions were gathered together. He was getting back into the spiritual zone of recognizing who he was and where he was and what he had been and what he wanted to become.

It was upon this third day, after the seas had been gathered together, that God commanded the dry earth to bring forth grass and herbs and fruit trees. These were the lower forms of vegetable life and is, we say, unthinking and unconscious or unintelligible to its forms of life. This is a picture of the beginnings of those living forces in the conscience and the will and the desires of the heart in the processes of salvation. We are so marvelously constructed that we are not able to discern and analyze all the various elements in our moral and spiritual being. But after we have entered into the state of regeneration and received the enlightening power of the Holy Spirit, we are then able to look back and notice a great many things which took place in our soul while passing through repentance and the new birth which we could not recognize at the time we were passing through those conditions. There are forms of desires and affection that spring up in the soul of the true penitent which are not entirely spiritual on the one side, and they are not carnal on the other side, but are the movements of our natural human feelings, our natural affections and sympathies and the natural longings of the intellect after the things of God which form a lower type of religious life, corresponding to the formation of vegetables and trees in the natural world.

4. The fourth day the Lord said, "Let there be lights in the firmament of heaven to divide the day from the night; and let them be for signs, and for seasons, and for days and years." And He made two great lights to rule the day and the night, and He made the stars also. Here we have for the first time in the process of creation the distinct formation and revelation of the sun, moon and stars as specific bodies of light. Now while it was true that light was the first thing in creation after the formation of the original atoms, yet it was not until the fourth day that light was manifested in distinct orbs or shining globes.

This corresponds exactly with the fourth step in the process of the new creation and forming a believer in Christ Jesus. The sun corresponds with the person of the Lord Jesus, and the moon corresponds with the Christian church in the new creation, and the stars correspond to individual believers; so that we see a perfect agreement between the orbs of light in the old material creation and the distinct forms and bodies of light in the new and spiritual creation.

A day with the Lord is a thousand years, but a day with man is twenty-four hours; and so Moses tells us, referring to the past creation, that a day with the Lord is a thousand years (Psalm 90 : 4). And then St. Peter tells us, referring to the judgment day, that a day with the Lord is a thousand years. Thus Moses, referring to the past, and Peter referring to the future, both declare that with God a day is a thousand years. Now in conformity with these statements, the Son of God was not born in human flesh and openly manifested

20

as an individual incarnate God to this world until the fourth day; that is, the fourth thousand years of human history. Just as light was in the universe before the sun was formed on the fourth day, so the light of God was in all human history for four thousand years, from Adam to Jesus. But the close of the fourth thousand years of human history, that is, the fourth day in the great work of the new creation, the Son of God was revealed as a man and became the Light of this world. Shortly after, the church was formed and manifested, corresponding with the moon, and the individual saints were formed in the Christian dispensation, corresponding with the stars. All this took place at the close of the fourth day, that is, the fourth thousand years.

It is impossible that all these things should have taken place by chance. The perfection of God's plans and works burst out around us everywhere when we study them in the light of His Word and providence and when we form them into an arrangement of harmony.

This also corresponds with the fact of the new birth, that when the penitent receives Christ as a present Saviour from all his sins, there is manifested to the eye of his faith the person of the Lord Jesus as an individual Saviour, bearing all his sins on the cross. There is light given to the sinner in his first conviction, but that light is not formed into an individual personal revelation of the Lord Jesus as a Saviour until the act of saving faith, and then Christ appears to the eye of faith as a distinct orb of saving grace, corresponding to the fact of the visible sun being manifested on the fourth day of creation.

5. On the fifth day of creation there was formed all manner of living creatures in the sea and fowls of the air. This also corresponds with the fact that following the act of saving faith in Christ, the affections of the heart and the mind are filled with the effects and fruits of the new birth; for there is a complete change in the natural affections and in the thoughts of the mind, showing how the new birth is communicated to all the feelings and sentiments of the soul in all the relationships of the domestic life, the social relations, the opinions of the mind, the thoughts and imaginations of the intellect, which correspond to the fowls that fly in the air.

6. It was on the sixth day of creation that God made all kinds of cattle and beasts of the earth, and concluded with the making of man in His own image and giving him dominion and lordship over all the world and everything in it. This corresponds with the fact that the new creation in the soul must be concluded with the formation of Christ in the heart and the enthronement of the Lord Jesus over the whole being as Lord of all. The new birth is not an ultimate thing in itself, but through out all Scripture, and especially in the Epistles, we are taught that after the new birth has taken place in man's moral nature there must be the enthronement of the Lord Jesus Christ taking possession of the whole heart and soul and extending the boundaries of His perfect love throughout the whole man. It is a great mistake, both in Bible teaching and in experience, to think that the forgiveness of sins or a change of heart is an ultimate matter in the Christian life, for always and forever in the Christian religion Jesus must be the ultimate one, and the new birth is a preparation for the perfect inward manifestation of the Lord Jesus and His complete dominion in the heart. All the steps that a soul takes in the process of salvation, from repentance to the perfection of love, are but preparatory to divine union, to that perfect heart-oneness which God has planned to exist between Christ and the believer.

Thus we see in the various six days of creation a perfect outline of the process of the new creation in causing the natural darkness of the sinner to pass away and bringing the believer into the state of a full believer and state of divine oneness with Christ, which culminates in that blessed God-Man having dominion over all things in our being to the glory of God the Father.

5

Evening and Morning

As we study God's first words in the book of Genesis we need to go a little slow and put things together in a thoughtful and prayerful manner, and compare Scripture with Scripture from the beginning to the end of the Bible, in order that we may be most powerfully impressed with the utterances that come out of the divine mind. We shall find the key to all Scripture in the book of Genesis. Infidels always begin by attacking this book of Genesis, and yet they themselves do not know why such is the case, for they are not aware that their minds are acting under the guidance of Satan or of some demon, and the Devil knows that if he can discredit the book of Genesis, it will undermine every other book in the Bible; but to a true believer, led and illuminated by the Holy Spirit, the book of Genesis blazes with transcendent light in every direction, whether toward God or toward man, and no part of the Bible is more solid than the words we find in this first book of Scripture.

Have you ever noticed that in the first chapter of Genesis, in connection with each of the six days of creation, every day concludes with the remark that the evening and morning made the day? "The evening and the morning were the first day," and so on to the last "the evening and the morning made the sixth day." Every uninspired man would have naturally written the morning and the evening made the day, but God speaks just the opposite of the natural man, and He always puts the evening first and the morning last. This is God's first word revealing the fact that He always works from darkness to light, from sin to holiness, from sorrow to joy, from poverty to wealth, from weakness to strength, from the natural to the supernatural, from the earthly to the heavenly, from the uncertain to the true, from doubt to faith, from the human to the divine, from the temporal to the eternal, from the cursing to the blessing, from the mortal to the immortal. The wheels of God never turn backward, but always and forever, from world's end to world's end, His ever blessed footsteps march onward and upward in the revelations of Himself in His dealings with His creatures in the steps of His great salvation. It is enough to thrill our minds with everlasting gladness to watch the ways of God, to notice the movements of His hands and the onward sweep of His government.

We notice in the second verse of Genesis there was darkness upon the face of the deep, and then we notice that the Spirit of God moved upon that darkness and out of it came light, and out of the light came the sun, moon, and stars. Now if you will go through the entire Bible you will find that we have here the key to all God's dealings. When Abraham had his great vision of sorrow and darkness recorded in Genesis 15, when he saw a representation of the sufferings of his posterity in the land of Egypt, we read that there was a smoking furnace and a burning lamp that passed between the pieces of his sacrifice at the time when he felt a great horror of darkness resting upon his soul. There was first the horror of darkness, a picture of the terrible bondage of his children in Egypt; and then the smoking furnace, a type of intense trial and the groaning and praying of his posterity to God for deliverance; and then came the burning lamp, the bright shining light, representing the deliverance of the Hebrews and their being formed into a nation and becoming the shining lamp among the nations, to illuminate mankind on the things of God.

Then in the case of Jacob, through that long, dark night in which the Angel of Jehovah wrestled with him, we notice the struggle through the dark night, but when the day was breaking over the eastern hills and the light was spread around him he obtained the blessing and went forward in perfect victory over his brother and over all his enemies.

And then we notice in the life of Moses how he fled from Egypt in distress of mind and had forty years of the testing of his faith, and then came the glorious vision of God at the burning bush and power and victory in the deliverance of his people.

24

In the case of David who for fifteen years was chased as an animal over mountains and amid the rocks and oftentimes there was only a step between him and death, yet at last the day broke, the enemies were slain and scattered and he ascended to his throne to feed the people of God with the bread of knowledge.

In the case of Mordecai we notice first the awful oppression under the wicked Haman and his going out in the street with a loud and bitter cry because of the death sentence, and then the marvelous and instantaneous change of affairs in the downfall of Haman and the enthronement of Mordecai, ruling the vast nation in tranquility and justice.

Then we see in the case of the blessed Jesus the storm that gathered around His closing days on earth and the darkness and agony of the garden, and on the cross the supernatural darkness in which He died, and then three days after the glorious sunburst of resurrection and power and honor and victorious ascension to the right hand of God.

And in the coming tribulation there will be a period of unparalleled agony upon this earth which will terminate with that dark day when the sun will not shine and the moon will turn to blood, and in that darkness the antichrist and his armies will go down unto death or the lake of fire; and it is followed at once with the great day-break of Millennial glory and Christ standing on Mt. Olivet and reigning in Jerusalem and filling the world with righteousness as waters fill the sea.

And how true all this is in our individual lives. What darkness and sorrow there is to our souls when we are brought under conviction for our sins, and then we drink the wormwood of penitential sorrow and eat the bitter herbs like the Hebrews at the time of the Passover; but this is followed by the sweetness of pardon and the light of divine love that springs up in the heart.

And also there are seasons of trial, sorrow, trouble, which often come to God's people, causing them to weep with anguish, to agonize in prayer, to wait with long patience for the mercy of God, for deliverance, for comfort; but at last to those who wait with patient faith, the shadows flee away, and His loving providence opens like a great sunflower upon the soul, the storms pass away, and the tranquility and sweetness of God's fatherly care break out around the true believer and he then sees that God has made everything work for his good.

In the case of Satan and sinners, they always go from bad to worse. The natural man has his good things first and his bad things last, but Jesus always plans to have the best wine at the last.

When we put all these things together and see how this is the way God works forever and forever in the creation of the world, in the plan of redemption, in the arrangements of providence, in our individual lives, these things furnish us with an infallible proof that God is always true to His word, and always is better and better to our souls as we go on in our heavenly journey.

After six thousand years of human history, after all the dealings that God has had with His people in all generations, it still comes out in the end just exactly as we have it in God's first words; it is always the evening first and the morning last. Thus we can take heart and know for a surety that if we identify ourselves with the blessed Lord Jesus, we are going on forever and forever toward an eternal morning, a morning of light and glory that will never be followed by a sunset.

6

The Image of God

When God said, "Let us make man in our image and after our likeness," what do you suppose He really meant? Does God have an image for sure and a real likeness? Shall we go by the Bible, or shall we go by a man-made theology? Human theology teaches us that God has no image, but the Bible denies it; so you can take your choice between Scripture or human theology.

There is not one word in the Bible which teaches that God has no image. On the other hand, there are many Scriptures which teach that God has a form, an image, a likeness, and that image is revealed in Scripture. We are commanded to make no image or likeness of God, but that does not prohibit God from making an image of Himself. Every time that a man attempts to make an image of God he makes a lie, something that is false, something that dishonors God. When God makes an image of Himself, He makes something that is true, that is worthy of the divine being, something that always conduces to God's glory.

It is true that God is an infinite Spirit, existing from eternity to eternity and possessing every moral and spiritual perfection which it is possible for the human mind to conceive, and also many perfections which lie beyond the thinking of the human mind. In this respect God's essence and presence through all space and through all eternity does not have any definite form or shape that we can conceive of. While this is true, it is also true that when God manifests Himself and reveals His personality, His word, His character, His conduct, He takes a form which is in harmony with the glory of His infinite nature.

We may say that electricity pervades every drop of water and every atom of earth and air, and in that respect it has no special form or shape, but at the same time wherever electricity manifests itself in lightning or a storm of fire it takes a form and a shape in its manifestation. Now this illustrates the nature of God, that in one sense He may exist through all space without form, but whenever God reveals Himself to angels or men He takes a form, and hence He has an image in His manifestation.

Now our next thought is, what is that form or image? We do not have to go far to find the answer in Scripture. That image is the Lord Jesus Christ, the God-Man, the man Christ Jesus. But where did God get the shape of a man, with his head and body and arms, legs and feet and face and with the marvelous make-up of the human faculties? The answer is, He got it from His own self in the past eternity, millions of ages before Adam was made or before men walked on this earth. From eternity the infinite God generated His only begotten Son in His bosom and that Son was God's manifestation to the universe of His personality and character. And that Son had the same form back in eternity in the bosom of God that He had when He walked on this earth and was crucified on the cross and ascended to the right hand of God, and the same form that He will have when He returns in radiant glory to chain the Devil and reign on the earth and govern the universe throughout everlasting ages that are to come.

The form of the Lord Jesus Christ was from eternity, before ever He made Adam. And hence when He said, "Let us make man in our image," He fashioned the first man of the human race according to the pattern and personal shape of the ever blessed Son of God. Jesus said to the Jews, "Before Abraham was, I am," for He existed before Abraham and before Adam. The first time that the Son of God ever manifested Himself to the firstborn angels He had the same form that He had when He made Adam and that He has today at the right hand of the Father.

There are some catechisms in which the question is put about man being made in the image of God, "What did the image consist of?" The answer is, "It consisted of righteousness and true holiness." That is true, but that is not all the truth by a long way. In the creation of Adam as recorded in God's first words there is nothing said about righteousness or true holiness, but the language is, "Let us make man in our image, and let him have dominion."

When we put together all the Bible teaching we find that Adam, when he was formed, was in the image of God. Just as the eternal Father contained within Himself from eternity the divine Son and the Holy Spirit, so Adam, when he was first formed, contained within himself Eve and the child. Eve was formed out of one of Adam's ribs. She was in Adam from the time Adam was made, but she was not manifested or revealed as a distinct person until God put Adam to sleep and took his rib and built Eve; but none the less she was in Adam from the beginning of his existence. Eve was not born, she was not generated, but she proceeded from the body of Adam. In like manner the Holy Ghost was not born or generated, and Jesus tells us that the Holy Ghost proceeds from the Father. The Holy Ghost is an eternal divine person flowing out from the Father, without beginning, without ending.

The child begotten by Adam was in his body from the time of his creation and hence was as old as Adam, of the same nature and substance and character and attributes. The child was begotten and born, a thing that cannot be applied either to Adam or to Eve. And here we have a perfect image of the triune God, the three divine Persons, and also the mode of their existence.

There is only one God, but in that Godhead there is only one Father, and out from that Father proceeds the Holy Spirit, without being born or begotten, and out from that Father comes the eternal Son, Who is begotten and born. This is a perfect image of Almighty God, Father, Son, and Holy Spirit, one God, one substance, one eternity, one nature, one glory, but three distinct and separate persons.

This is not all. In the human family there never can be but three relationships without starting another family. There were Adam, and Eve and the child. It does not matter whether it applies to one child or other children, but these three primal relationships can never be increased without starting another family. So here we have another feature in the image of God. Hence there never can be any other God than the God we have revealed in the Bible; there never can be but one eternal Father, one eternal Son and one eternal Holy Spirit.

Here is a fountain of everlasting joy for our souls, that we have a God that never can change, never can be false, never can commit sin, a God Whose infinite perfections fill eternity and all space and fill our little lives. These great radiant divine perfections flow around us by day and by night, from the beginning of our lives on to the end, like great bright shining waters in which we can bathe our spirits by simple faith in spite of outward circumstances. And we can look forward to the everlasting ages that are to come and be glad that God has made a plan to recreate us in Christ Jesus, and restore that blessed image of Himself which was lost in the fall, and cause us to inherit in His image the very life and joy of God Himself.

Thus we have in the first chapter of Genesis God's first word about His image. And that first word holds good throughout all Scripture and will reach its highest consummation in the first resurrection, when we shall be entirely like the Son of God, for "we shall see Him as He is."

7

The First Plan of the Kingdom

We are told in the Apocrypha that God does nothing except He does it by time and number and measure. Everything that God does is according to some pattern which exists in the divine mind. Hence when He arranged the creation of the world and man He formed a plan of the kingdom which He would set up on this earth, of which Adam and Eve were to be the co-regents over all the lower creation, and that they should bring forth a race of rulers that should have dominion over the material universe. The first word concerning this divine plan is found in the language, "And God said, Let us make man in our image, after our likeness: and let them have dominion over the fish of the sea, and over the fowl of the air, and over the cattle, and over all the earth, and over every creeping thing that creepeth upon the earth" (Gen. 1:26).

Have you noticed that in these words the first word God ever uttered in connection with making man was that of dominion, which gives the primeval thought in the mind of God that the human race was designed to be a generation of rulers over all the lower works of God? The holiness of Adam and his longevity and all the elements of his character as a child of God were certainly included, but they were not mentioned, and the supreme thought was that of dominion. The same idea was expressed just after the flood, when Noah and his family came out of the ark, when God said to Noah, "Be fruitful, and multiply, and replenish the earth. And the fear of you and the dread of you shall be upon every beast of the earth, and upon every fowl of the air, upon all that moveth upon the earth, and upon all the fishes of the seas; into your hand are they delivered" (Gen. 9:2). Here we see the second beginning of the race and the second expression of the supreme thought of being a ruler over all the lower creation and every form of living creature in the world.

In the 8th Psalm David repeats the same thought of the rulership of man over all the lower creation when he says: "Thou hast made man a little lower than the angels, and hast crowned him with glory and honor. Thou madest him to have dominion over the works of thy hands; thou hast put all things under his feet: All sheep and oxen, and the beasts of the field, and fowl of the air and fish of the sea." This proof is repeated over and over again in many forms throughout all Scripture. In the closing words of Revelation we have the same thought when John says he saw thrones and the martyred saints sat on them, and the power to judge the world was given unto them, and they lived and reigned with Christ a thousand years (Rev. 20:4-6).

Jesus tells us that at the judgment day He will say to the righteous, "Come, ye blessed of my Father, inherit the kingdom prepared for you from the foundation of the world" (Matt. 25:34). Now just look at it, that the kingdom which was arranged at the creation of Adam has never been changed and never will change. It goes on persistently in the purpose of God throughout all the generations of mankind and the different dispensations of human history, and comes out in the end of human probation in its full and perfect realization when the resurrected and glorified children of God are to come into their inheritance and take the dominion over all the works of God just exactly as it was planned in the first chapter of Genesis.

This proves that God's plans are as perfect at the beginning as they are at the end, and that His words are so absolutely pure and correct that they never change, never break down, never fail of accomplishment, and that as the ages go by they are simply enlarged into a wider application.

The next thought in connection with this plan of the kingdom is to study the creation of Adam as the king of the world. "And the Lord God formed man of the dust of the ground and breathed into his nostrils the breath of life; and man became a living soul" (Gen. 2:7). How many thousands of times foolish skeptics and poor, ignorant, depraved men have tried to change these words of the living God. Some so-called scientists that know nothing of the living God or the Bible have taught that man's body was an evolution from some lower forms of animal life, but this theory is absolutely contradicted by the laws of all nature, by the Word of God, and by all human history and the investigations of science. There is no such thing as one species jumping over its boundaries and forming another species, for God ordained that every animal and tree and plant should bring forth seed and reproduction after its own kind. From that day to this no species of animal or tree has ever leaped the bounds of its own nature to bring forth a monstrosity of some other species.

On the other hand, those who have accepted only the teaching of materialism have denied the true Bible doctrines of the human soul. The Seventh Day Adventists and the Millenial Dawn teaching assert that man does not possess an ever living human spirit, but that a human being consists of nothing but a material body and the breath of atmosphere that is in the lungs the same as any lower animal has. But in these first words concerning the formation of man we see plainly that the body was formed out of the dust and that the soul was formed out of the divine breath or the divine Spirit, proving that the spirit of man is something separate and distinct from the body. While the body is taken from the dust of the earth, the spirit of man is formed by the Holy Ghost.

The Apostle Paul shows us the contrast between the first man Adam and the second man who was made a quickening, that is, a life-giving Spirit. The living soul is a soul or a spirit-man within the body that is to exist forever and ever, without one single hint of annihilation in the whole Bible. But Adam had no power to communicate life to the dead. On the other hand, Christ was a quickening Spirit, that is, He had power to communicate life unto the dead, an intimate, divine authority over creation by which He can raise the dead and regenerate a fallen, sinful man and put divine life in him, which distinguishes Him as infinitely superior to a natural man.

Another fact concerning the original plan for the kingdom is that Adam was to propagate a race of rulers. The idea of rulership is the most dominant thought in all the Bible respecting the creation of man, both in his original creation and in the plan of the redemption. When the day of rewards shall come, Jesus says that He will say to His faithful servants, "Thou hast been faithful over a few things,

I will make thee ruler over many things." And then again He says in the parable of the pounds that the servant who had ten pounds should have authority over ten cities, and the servant who had five should have authority over five cities. And then in the messages that Jesus gives to the seven churches He says: "He that overcometh, and keepeth my works unto the end, to him will I give power (or authority) over the nations: And he shall rule them with a rod of iron; as the vessels of a potter shall they be broken to shivers: even as I received of my Father." Just exactly as the eternal Father appointed His Son, the Lord Jesus, to be the supreme King over the entire universe, over all worlds and angels and men and demons, so in like manner Jesus affirms He will appoint to His overcoming servants authority over the nations that will live on this earth in the coming age, or after dispensations, as well as authority over all the lower animals and the material things and laws of nature.

All these Scriptures have been so long perverted by false teaching, that they are to be fulfilled only in a metaphorical or spiritual sense. Thus the Word of God has almost ceased to have any real power upon the minds of professing Christians, because instead of taking the Word of God in its true, literal meaning, it has been whittled off into thin shavings of ghost smoke.

The Salvation that we receive through our divine Saviour, consisting in its entirety of the new birth, sanctification, and the resurrection from the dead, this salvation is only preparatory to the Kingdom of Heaven which is to be perfected and manifested in absolute reality and glory in the age to come. The Church has mostly been taught simply the rudiments of Bible doctrine; that if sinners will come to Jesus and repent and receive Christ and go to Heaven when they die, that that is a finality. Millions and millions of church members have never heard any Bible teaching that goes beyond simply being forgiven their sins and getting to Heaven when they die. And hence the vast plan of God concerning mankind. concerning the children of God. concerning the great kingdom that He planned originally and will consummate in the end, has never dawned upon the minds of but few Christians.

Another fact is, we must understand the expression where it is said in the Scriptures, referring to God's making of man. "I have said that ye are gods." Now in what sense can it be true that God made man to be a god? The words can only be understood by studying these passages in which God created Adam to be a ruler over all things in this world. God planned that Adam should be a god to all the lower creations, and that all animals and fishes and birds should worship him and obey him and honor him up to their capacity, as he, in his capacity, should worship Jehovah and love and honor and obey Him. The lower animals have souls, but they do not have spirits. The lower animals can love and hate and learn and obey man, but they do not possess a spiritual conscience, they do not have an inward spirit nature by which they can touch God or know God, and hence man is to them a god. If Adam had never sinned, all the lower animals would have been his loving and obedient subjects and would have worshiped him, but when Adam became a sinner he lost his dominion, his scepter, and his throne, and then the lower animals turned against him. But this perfect dominion is to be restored in the resurrection of the just, and the glorified sons of God and all the lower creation will be obedient and subservient to the glorified saints in the time of what the apostle calls the restitution of all things.

Again, not only did God plan to make Adam the king of the lower animals, but also over the forces of nature, such as air and water and the natural elements in the physical world. Jesus when He walked on the sea did not do so merely because He was God, but by virtue of His being a perfect, sinless man, the second Adam, and by virtue of His natural dominion over the laws of nature. He caused Peter to walk on the sea, and although it was only a short distance, yet nonetheless he walked on the sea, which was a prophetic indication of what will come to the sons of God in their glorified state when they are risen from the dead.

Another fact in connection with this kingdom was that Adam, as the first appointed ruler of the world, was divinely inspired to understand all the laws of nature and the secrets in all the lower animals, so that when God allowed him to give names to all the lower animals, he gave each creature an appropriate name, corresponding exactly with the make-up and instincts of the animals. The names Adam gave to them were exactly indicative of their make-up, proving that he was a divinely inspired scientist.

And also Adam was an inspired prophet and foretold the facts concerning the human species which have persisted down to the present hour. When he said that a man would leave his father and mother and cleave unto his wife, he certainly spoke by the Holy Ghost as a prophet, for he had never left his father and mother to cleave to his wife, and how could he know that such would be the case throughout all the generations of mankind except by the inspiration of the Spirit of God? Luke tells us that the coming of Christ and His kingdom and the reign of Jesus on the throne of David had been prophesied ever since the world was made, which proves that Adam was a prophet and that he foretold to his posterity not only the first coming, but also the second coming of Jesus to reign as a King over this world.

Now only think of it, that when we give ourselves up to Jesus and receive Him as a personal Saviour and are born again, we enter into this vast original purpose of the infinite God and become members of that divine kingdom which was originated from the foundation of the world. And if we are loyal servants to Jesus and are true to the trust He puts in our hands, we are to be rewarded by having a place of rulership in that kingdom which was started at the foundation of the world.

8

The First Bride

Just as God's plan for the kingdom was as perfect at the beginning of the Bible as at the end of it, so God had a plan for the Bride of Christ, and that plan was instituted at the creation of Adam and Eve and has remained unchanged throughout all generations, and will be consummated in the winding up of human probation. "And the Lord God caused a deep sleep to fall upon Adam, and he slept; and he took one of his ribs, and closed up the flesh instead thereof; and the rib which the Lord God had taken from man, made he a woman, and brought her unto the man. And Adam said, This is now bone of my bones, and flesh of my flesh; she shall be called Woman, because she was taken out of Man" (Gen. 2:21-23). The way God formed a wife for Adam is exactly the way He is now forming a bride for His only begotten Son. This plan of forming the first bride was eternal in the mind of God, and that plan has never been changed and never will be changed, and forms a perfect revelation of the things concerning Christ and the church of the firstborn.

1. In the deep sleep that God put upon Adam we see a prophecy of the death of Christ and how His body was put to sleep, and out from the death of Christ there is formed the Bride of the Lamb as definitely as Eve was formed from the rib of Adam. Our salvation is procured only by the death of Jesus. How little this Scripture truth is understood by many who think they are Christians. We are not saved by the example of Christ, nor by His birth, nor by His miracles, but most emphatically and only by His death; and if you will take all the Scriptures say about the death of Christ, you will find they affirm most positively that we are saved only by His death. If Jesus had suffered for us ten times more than He did suffer and yet had not died, we could never have been saved. It was not only His sufferings, but His suffering unto death that constituted the redemption for human

beings. And so in the deep sleep that God gave Adam we have the foreshadowing of that deep sleep in death that Jesus entered into, out of which comes our salvation and the formation of His church and His bride.

2. In forming a bride for Adam out of his own bones and flesh we see a prophecy of the perfect oneness between Christ and His true church. It is not a metaphorical oneness or a legal oneness, but most emphatically a oneness of nature, of life, for the apostle says we are members of His bones and of His flesh and of His body. The union of a true believer with Jesus is not a mechanical union, but a living oneness, as the branch with the vine, as the finger with the hand, a oneness of life and nature and character.

3. In forming a bride out of Adam's rib, we get another revelation concerning her rank as his companion. God did not take a bone out of Adam's foot to be under him, nor a bone out of his head to have authority over him, but a rib from his side, to be his equal, his companion, his joint partner in life and authority. This same truth holds good in the formation of a company of chosen saints in all ages to be the Bride of Jesus Christ. God did not take the entire body of Adam, but only a chosen part of that body, a special selection from a certain part of the body, which was full of prophetic instruction.

The teaching that the Jews are to form the Bride of Christ is utterly unscriptural, because St. Paul speaks of espousing certain Gentile Christians to Christ to be His wife. And again, all through Scripture there are many prophetic parables of an elect Jew taking a wife from the Gentiles, as in the case of Moses, Joseph, Naashon, Solomon, and others. And Isaiah prophesies that there will be more members of the Bride of Christ from among the Gentiles than from among the Jews. Israel was the earthly wife of Christ in the old dispensation, but when a woman kills her husband it certainly divorces him from that woman. But the Bride of Christ is to be a heavenly bride, composed of resurrected and glorified saints.

It is also unscriptural to teach that all who are saved will form the Bride of Christ, for every single Scripture bearing on this subject goes to show that the Bride is a selected number from the countless millions who are saved. If we search into every Scripture bearing on the subject of the Bride of Christ, we will find that in all cases it is a rib taken from the heart or the center of the body. The twelve tribes of Israel all belonged to God, but He selected the tribe of Levi to be the holy tribe that should furnish the priests and the teachers and religious guides, and be the church of the Firstborn. In Egypt God claimed the first born of every family of the Hebrews, but in the wilderness He told Moses He would take the tribe of Levi to be to Him for the firstborn. Hence in all Scripture the church of the Firstborn does not include all who are saved, but corresponds exactly with the word of God to Moses that the tribe of Levi should be for the firstborn. The apostle, in the 12th of Hebrews, speaks of all who are saved as composing "the general assembly" or the universal gathering of the saved ones, and then he speaks of "the church of the Firstborn," proving positively that the church of the Firstborn is not identical with "the universal gathering."

Now look at it: of the twelve tribes of Jacob, Levi was not the first son or the last one, but the third son; that is, the rib, near the center of the twelve tribes. When God selected our earth as the planet on which His Son should be incarnated, He did not select Mercury at the head of the solar system, or Neptune at the foot of the solar system, but He selected our earth, the third planet in the system, that is, the rib near the heart of the system. Do you think that that happened by chance? If so, you have never yet got hold of the great thought of God's creation or His plan in all His ways.

When God selected Palestine as the home for the twelve tribes and the place where His Son should be born, you see He did not choose the birth place of His Son in Lapland, at the top of the world, nor South Africa, at the foot of the world, but He chose the land of Canaan, the rib, the heart of all the various portions of the earth.

King David describes the royal bride in Psalm 45, but in that Psalm he mentions four classes of those who are saved in the kingdom; the honorable women, who are one company, and the daughter of Tyre, which represents another company, and then the virgins or her companions, which are another company. But over and above all these companies of saved ones he speaks of the king's daughter as sitting at the king's right hand, dressed in the gold of Ophir, and all her garments are of wrought gold, and she is superior to all other companies of the redeemed.

Also in the sixth chapter of the Song of Solomon there is a description of the various companies that are in the kingdom, consisting of four great ranks, for he says there are "three score queens" which form one company and "four score concubines" which form another company, and "virgins without number" which form another company. But above all these he says "my dove, my undefiled is the choice one, or the elect one of her mother, and this choice one is the bride."

When Jesus explained how His disciples were so happy in His companionship in contrast with John's disciples, who were sad, He said, "My disciples are the children of the bridechamber." And while John's disciples were religious men and most certainly on the way to Heaven, and among those that were saved, yet they did not take rank with those other disciples which He declares were children of the bridechamber.

Thus if we study every Scripture in the Bible on the subject of the Bride, as well as God's plan for our earth in the solar system and God's plan for the land of Canaan in the geography of the earth, we find everything in the world points one way—that the Bride of Christ is the rib taken from the great body, is a chosen company of devoted souls in all generations who are more closely united to Christ than others are. It is this company that constitutes the elect wife of the King of the world, and the company that will be His helpmeet and His co-regents in the administration of His kingdom in the ages that are to come.

Another fact we must not forget is that after the fall there was a prophecy in the second name that was given to Adam's wife concerning things to come. Her first name was Woman, the Hebrew word being "Ishsha," which simply means the female man. But after the fall, when God gave the promise of redemption and a new creation and that the seed of the woman should bruise Satan's head, then she obtained the name of Eve. The word "Eve" signifies the mother of life, or more literally, the mother of the living one, that is the mother of the incarnate Son of God.

The name Eve occurs only four times in the Bible and the number four is always that number indicative of the world, the earth, or mankind. So that while Ishsha was her natural name, Eve is her redemption name. As there was to be a second man to be the Saviour of the world, so there was to be a second wife of redeemed and glorified saints to form the helpmeet for the second Man, and as the first Eve was taken as a rib from Adam's body, so the second Eve, the glorified woman of the elect saints, should be taken from the heart of the Lord Jesus.

Thus we see that the first words God ever spoke regarding a bride for Adam have never been changed, but only enlarged and extended into the new creation.

9

The First Steps to Sin

In the first and second chapters of Genesis we have God's first words in relation to creation and in relation to the plan of God's kingdom, and in relation to the formation and dignity of the first pair and their rank in the creation. With the beginning of the third chapter we have the first words respecting the temptation of Eve and the fall, and the various steps by which our first parents fell from their natural state of holiness into a condition of sin. These first words in regard to the steps of the fall reveal to us the same order in the steps to sin that have taken place in all generations with reference to temptation and the fall of people into the ways of evil.

We learn from the Bible that Satan was the first sinner in the universe, for Jesus says he was a liar and the father of lies. Hence we see in the third of Genesis that sin and temptation came from Satan. It would seem that Satan's plan was to imitate God by incarnating himself in the serpent and using the serpent as a medium of communication with the first pair, and also as the instrument of leading our first parents into sin. It is evident that originally the serpent walked erect, for when he was cursed he had to crawl prone on the ground, showing that that condition was not his original state. We are also told that the serpent was the wisest of all the beasts of the field and was endowed naturally with the most intelligence and the highest sensibility of any of the lower creatures. Satan took hold upon the serpent because he was superior to all other animals in order to more effectually tempt Eve to commit sin.

It would seem from some other passages in the Bible that before the world was made God had proclaimed to the angels His purpose to incarnate His Son, and we are told by the apostle that when that plan was made known, God commanded that all the angels should worship His incarnate Son. It would seem that Lucifer, who was probably the highest of the angels, refused to worship the incarnate Son of God, because he wanted to occupy the place of prime minister of the universe himself. Because of this pride in him he lost his place in Heaven and fell into the condition of the first sinner, by which he was turned into the Devil. Now if we analyze the temptation and fall of Eve, we will see the following points:

1. The very first step in the temptation and fall was that she listened to the words of Satan as spoken to her through the mouth of the serpent. And the serpent said: "Ye shall not surely die: for God doth know that in the day ye eat thereof, then your eyes shall be opened, and ye shall be as gods, knowing good and evil." This was the first lie that was ever spoken to a human being in this world, and when Eve listened to that lie, that formed the initial step in her temptation and downfall. I have remarked in a previous chapter that the spoken word always comes first, and then the act comes afterward. That truth is illustrated in this account of the temptation, for we see that Eve first listened to the serpent and then the act of disobedience came afterward. It was believing the words of Satan that constituted the germ of temptation and sin. The first sin always consists in believing a lie, or in perverting the truth, or in the effort to make a lie seem true, which is all the same thing.

The Apostle Peter tells us that we are to escape or be delivered from the evil in the world by believing God's promises. Just as believing a lie was the first step to sin, so it is by believing God's precious promises of truth that we are delivered from sin. The doubt in the heart or the faith in the heart is always the first germ that produces evil or good. It is sometimes said it does not matter what people believe if they only live right. Such a remark can only be spoken by an ignoramus, because it is in the nature of things that we live according to our faith. If anyone believes a lie he will live a lie, and the only way to live the truth is to believe the truth, for it is always true forever and ever that character is the product of faith. Nobody can live any better than he believes. So the first step to the fall of Eve was listening to a lie and putting confidence in the words of Satan.

2. The woman saw the tree. She evidently not only looked at the tree, but fastened her gaze upon it, and the longer she looked the more beautiful the tree and the fruit seemed to grow upon her mind. First there was an admission of falsehood through the ear gate, and then came an appeal through the eye gate.

3. She saw that the tree was good for food. Here was an appeal to one of the natural appetites of the body. The appetite of hunger in itself is not sin, nor even a temptation; but when the thought is entertained in the mind of gratifying the appetite in an unlawful way, then there is aroused the temptation which, if not turned away from, will lead to sin.

4. She saw that the fruit of the tree was pleasant to the eyes. Here was the calling forth of another sensation in the mind in addition to that of natural hunger, for there was the awakening of the sensation of the beautiful, and the attraction to one's mental taste and imagination. This is exactly the same process of temptation in all generations as the process takes place in the human mind.

5. She also saw that the fruit was desirable to make one wise. Here was a still further step in the process of temptation, because there was awakened a mental ambition after unlawful knowledge, the desire to penetrate into the secrets of God or that intense awakening of the faculty of curiosity to know things ahead of time that would conduce to vanity and pride and self-exaltation.

In every kind of temptation that the mind is subjected to there has to be the element of curiosity, and also that of intellectual pride or ambition to know more than others know, or to get hold of some secret above our station and above our natural ability. You will notice that all the wicked cults of lying religions and systems of fraud lay claim to extraordinary wisdom and profess to know secrets away beyond the plain revelations of God. This is only in keeping with this original temptation, that the forbidden fruit had a fascination in it and a promise to make one very wise.

6. The next step was the yielding of the will, for we read that she took of the fruit and did eat. At this point in the process the mental faculties had gone through their appropriate steps of exercise leading up to the point of the consent of the will, and then followed the

overt act which was the embodiment of unbelief and disobedience.

There is another word that Eve mentioned in giving her account to God which we ought to put down in this connection. When she gave her account to God, she said that the serpent beguiled her and she did eat. But the word "beguile" signifies in the original that the serpent "made her forget," that is, that while the process of temptation was going on in her mind she was so excited and bewildered with the words of the serpent and the fascination of the fruit that for the time being she forgot the words of God. This is exactly what takes place in countless thousands of cases. When people begin to listen to the tempter and entertain the temptation, the mind becomes so agitated and excited that, for the time being, the Word of God is forgotten and the memory is preoccupied with other things.

Now we see in this process that the action of the will is not the first step, but the last step in the process of committing sin. All the other steps, such as listening to a lie, gazing on the forbidden object, the ambition to be over wise, the intensifying of the natural appetites, these steps are preliminary to the decision of the will, which is the consummation of the temptation into sin.

7. The crowning act of the fall of Eve was communicating her sin to Adam, for it is said "she gave unto her husband and he did eat." There is something awfully contagious in sin and it has a terrible power of communicating itself, like an epidemic. Now just look at it: here we have the oldest account in all the world of temptation and sin, and by analyzing these words we get a perfect photograph and moving picture of the steps of the human mind in listening to temptation and falling into sin. These original words at the beginning of human history are as perfect as any process in all the succeeding centuries, and they describe the exact progress by which people in all generations are tempted and by which they fall.

10

The First Effects of Sin

In the third chapter of Genesis we have a description of the first effects of sin in the account of the fall of our first parents. The law of cause and effect has never been changed from the creation of the world, and this is just as true in the mental and moral nature of man as it is of the laws of the physical nature. Now let us notice what the first effects of sin were upon Adam and Eve.

1. They discovered that they were naked. I am convinced from the universal testimony of the Scriptures bearing on the subject that before Adam and Eve fell they were enveloped in a mantle of light and glory in such a way that they were not conscious of wearing any clothes and at the same time were not aware of being naked, for their bodies were enclosed in a mantle of light. In searching the Scriptures on this point, we are told that God covers Himself with light as a garment, and not one word can be found intimating that God is naked. And again, in every place in Scripture where the angels are revealed they are spoken of as wearing white garments, and not one word even hints at their being naked. And then all the Scriptures referring to the manifestation of the Son of God, either in the Old Testament or after His resurrection, speak of Him as being dressed in white and in long flowing garments down to His feet.

It is true that when Christ died on the cross He was stripped of His garments, but that was because He took the place of a sinner, and on the cross God treated Him as sin; for He not only took the place of a sinner, but He took the place of sin. That accounts for the reason that the Father allowed Him to be stripped of His garments, and that is the reason why He cried "My God, why hast thou forsaken me?" because He then occupied the place of sin. Now, on the other hand, there is not one word in all the Bible about Satan or evil spirits having any clothes on, but every single passage bearing on that subject implies that Satan and wicked spirits are naked, for never is there one word about their having garments on them.

Now take all these facts and put them together and they show plainly that the first effect of the sin of our first parents was their discovery of their nakedness, which is the true condition of Satan and evil spirits. Before Adam sinned he was not aware of having a conscience, because the organ of conscience never comes into exercise except in connection with sin. If the human race had never committed sin, they would never have been aware of having a conscience, because conscience is an organ in man's moral nature that never reveals itself in a state of true holiness and righteousness, just as we are never aware of having the organs of a kidney or a liver or a lung as long as we are in a state of perfect health, for those organs perform their functions without any pain; but when they become diseased or in a wrong condition then we are conscious of having them.

So here we have the very first effect of sin in its operation in the human soul, the discovery of moral nakedness and the painful consciousness of an inward sense of corruption and shame and guilt.

2. The next effect of sin was an effort on the part of our first parents to conceal their shame and disgrace, and hence we read that they sewed fig leaves together and made themselves aprons. Here we see the effort of poor, sinful nature to save itself, to conceal the sins of shame and degradation by manufacturing a vegetable religion, a religion of nature as a means of their deliverance from guilt and shame. This effect of sin has descended through all the generations and is manifested throughout the world at the present time in the natural effort of the human mind to form a religion out of nature or natural elements as a substitute for genuine salvation.

The Seventh Day Adventists deny that they have an everlasting spirit nature within them—that they possess only a human body with breath in it. They think it is a sin to eat meat, and so they reduce everything in religion to materialism and on a level with the vegetable creation. They think that by eating vegetables and living on walnuts they will purify their physical system, and that is the height of their religious conception. And so they depend on a vegetable religion instead of a spiritual salvation that works through the blood of Christ by the power of the Holy Ghost.

Hence we see the effect of sin on Adam and Eve in their making fig leaves to be the first act of fallen man to form a religion out of nature without any atoning blood connected with it.

3. The next effect of sin was being afraid of God, for we read that they heard the voice of the Lord God walking in the garden in the cool of the day, and they hid themselves from the presence of the Lord among the trees of the garden. Before they sinned they had often met the personal Jehovah walking in the garden and having communion with them in most loving and tender fellowship, but the act of sin had produced within them the sense of shame and fear and guilt by which they had broken their fellowship with God; and so they were afraid to meet His face or hear His voice as in former times. This proves that sin in the very nature of things must produce banishment from God, not because God forsakes His creatures, but because His creatures are afraid of Him and flee from Him. The carnal mind is always afraid of holiness and is always uneasy in the presence of heavenly and holy manifestations. No sinner in his natural condition could ever be induced to go to heaven or to enter the precincts of holiness and heavenly glory. The very nature of sin is to flee from God and make for itself a miserable hell, hid away from the divine presence; and these first effects still persist in forming the conduct of all sinners down to the present hour.

4. The next effect of sin was self-defence, self-excuse, laying the blame on someone else! We see that Adam laid the blame on his wife, but indirectly he laid the blame on God, for he said: "The woman whom thou gavest to be with me, she gave me of the tree, and I did eat." You notice the words of Adam were in self-defense and to exonerate himself from any guilt in the transaction. And then Eve laid the blame on the serpent and excused herself from sin by saying she had been so bewildered, beguiled, and fascinated by what she had heard and seen that she forgot herself and did eat of the tree. This effect of sin has descended through every successive generation and today there is not a sinner or backslider in the whole world that does not defend himself or excuse his conduct or lay the blame on

some one else, showing that at the taproot of the sinner there is self-defense, self-excuse, for in the last analysis of all evil there is self.

All these points go to show that the human race has never changed since the fall of Adam, and that in itself and of itself it never will change. If the human race should live for millions of ages, it would still be the same character it was the very day that Adam and Eve partook of the forbidden fruit. Unless salvation comes from a higher source, there is nothing in the nature of man that can ever produce a change of heart or in any way lead the soul back to God.

11

The First Curse on Sin

If we put together the first curse God ever put on sin in this world as found in Genesis 3 and then the last curse as recorded in the closing chapters of Revelation, we find that they correspond exactly and agree in every particular, although thousands of years intervened between the first and the last. God does not grow, but is absolutely perfect from eternity, and His words and works are as perfect at the beginning as at the last. God's judgment on sin gives us a revelation of His true character, as radiant and bright in a display of His attributes as is His reward to the righteous for well-doing. God is just as good in punishing sin as He is in rewarding righteousness. If we saw the divine character and conduct as the angels do, we would rejoice in Him and love Him and appreciate Him just as much when He manifests His wrath against sin as when He manifests His love toward goodness. It is an infallible proof of the corruption of modern teaching when there is such an endeavor to do away with divine justice in punishing sin. All of the no-hell theology in this world is based on a positive hatred to God, the despising of His character and the antagonism of His law.

If you will study the words in the third of Genesis you will find a perfect picture of God's feelings and conduct towards sin, and also a panorama of God's actions in the various steps in which He punishes sin, which is well worth our knowledge.

1. We see God searching out the sinner. "And the Lord God called unto Adam, and said unto him, Where art thou?" This proves that God had not forgotten Adam and that God wanted to know where he was and all about his circumstances, and is an evidence that God still loved Adam, had not forsaken him, had not utterly turned him over into the hands of the Devil. The very fact that God searches out the sinner is a proof of divine love.

Adam has two names given to him. The first is Adam, a Hebrew word which signifies a man of the earth or a man formed of red clay. The second name is the Hebrew word "Ish," which always signifies the spirit man, the nobler man, the man that is capable of communion with God. When you read in the Old Testament the word "man," it is sometimes Adam in the original and sometimes Ish. The word "Adam" is used four hundred times in the Old Testament, and the word "Ish" is used eight hundred times in the Old Testament. When the word "man" is used in the low sense of being a sinner or a rebel, the original word is always "Adam." But when the word "man" is used in a high or good or noble sense, the original word is always "Ish," which in fact is one of the names given to Christ.

When the wicked men of Sodom are mentioned, the original word is "Adam," but when it speaks of Moses picking out brave soldiers to fight the Amalekites, the original word is "Ish." And so in every similar case in the Old Testament. Hence when Jehovah began to search out the man who had eaten the forbidden fruit, He called him Adam, the earthly or carnal man. And this furnishes us with an illustration of how God will search out the Adamic man in the last judgment.

2. After tracing the act of sin in Adam to the woman and then to the serpent, God then began to pronounce His judgments. And He began with the chief sinner, Satan, who had acted through the serpent. You notice that God began His judgment upon the chief sinner and from thence He descended down through man and into the products of the earth. There are degrees among sinners and so there are degrees in judgments; and this is brought out as perfectly in the first part of the Bible as in the last. When God judges the righteous before the judgment seat of Christ, He will begin with the best and wind up with the worst. On the other hand, when He judges the sinners, He begins with the worst and winds up with the least. With the righteous He begins by rewarding the ten-pounder, the best man first; but on the other hand, when He judges the wicked He begins with Satan, the serpent, and concludes with cursing the ground with briers and thorns. This gives us an insight into the ways

of God, that all His words and works are conducted with the infinite fitness of things.

3. Now notice that in judging the serpent God humiliated him down into the dust. The Lord said to the serpent, "Upon thy belly shalt thou go, and dust shalt thou eat." This proves that before that time the serpent had walked erect, and his curse consisted in being thrown down to crawl on the ground and take the form of the snake. The apostle tells us that the chief sin of the Devil was his pride, and the appropriate punishment for that sin was boundless humiliation and shame and degradation, to crawl on the earth in the form of a snake. And thus we see the absolute fitness of the kind of punishment God put on Satan, for the base humiliation was most fitting punishment for his boundless pride. It would seem from the last words in Revelation that throughout eternity the Devil will be compelled to take the form of a snake, and from various other Scriptures it would seem that the ultimate form of those who take sides with the Devil will be that of serpents. This is why John the Baptist spoke of the proud sinners of his day as a generation of serpents.

4. The next curse was upon the woman, which consisted in the multiplying of her conception and her sorrow in child bearing. If we knew all the facts in the case, we would see there was a perfect fitness between her sin and the kind of punishment that was placed upon her.

5. The next punishment was upon Adam, which consisted of hard work to make a living out of the ground. The curse on the woman was in the home life and in the bearing and raising of children, or multiplied sorrows and anxieties of motherhood. On the other hand, the curse upon man was out in the field, in the business life, in the struggle to make a living and in the difficulties connected with the culture of the earth. How significant it is that though six thousand years have passed away, these first words still are carried out among all the generations of mankind, and down to this hour this ancient form of the curse has never changed.

6. In the next place the curse descended into the earth, for we read that it should bring forth thorns and thistles. This proves that thorns and thistles were not a part of the original creation, but that

they were brought forth by the earth after the Fall. When Jesus returns to reign on the earth, this curse will be lifted and instead of the thorn, Isaiah tells us, there will spring up the fir tree, and instead of the brier there will spring up the myrtle tree. Another prophet tells us that righteousness shall drop down from the sky and truth shall spring out of the ground. We see in this original curse that man and the earth are so closely related to each other that they rise or fall in companionship. Everything in the lower creation, including animals and fishes and birds and all the vegetable kingdom, rises with man or falls with man, and God deals with the earth and man exactly alike.

7. Another item in the first judgment on sin is that of the two bruisings which are referred to in the conflict between the seed of the serpent and the seed of the woman. There is a spiritual seed as well as a fleshly and material seed. Jesus speaks of certain men as being children of the Devil; they have in their hearts the seed of the Satanic character. Again, we are told that the seed that Jesus plants is the Word of God; so that the Word of God is the divine seed, and the lie of Satan is the serpent's seed. Each of these kinds of seed are reproductive in the souls of men down through all generations. The serpent was to bruise Christ's heel and Christ was to bruise the serpent's head. Here we see there are two great bruisings to take place in this world between Jesus and Satan. Christ has already had His bruising on Calvary, when He was seized by the Devil's children and nailed to the cross, His precious humanity was bruised, that is the heel, the lower part of His nature, was bruised by Satan.

Now the time is drawing near when the Devil will get his bruising, for you must remember that Satan has never yet been bruised by the Lord Jesus, for he is still the prince of the powers of the air, he is still working with marvelous power in the world and among the sons of men. But when Jesus returns from the wedding banquet on high with His glorified saints, He will then seize upon the Devil and bind him and cast him into the abyss, that is, the hollow place at the center of the earth. That will be the time when Satan gets his bruising, and that bruising will be upon his head, upon the highest part of his nature.

The glorified saints will take part in that bruising of the Devil, for the Apostle Paul says "the God of peace will bruise Satan under the saints' feet after awhile." When Joshua slew the five kings on the day that the sun stood still, he brought those kings out from their hiding place, and made them lie down on the ground, and called for his captains to come and put their feet on the necks of those kings. At that time Joshua prophesied that thus would God do to all the enemies of the Lord's saints. So the day is coming when Jesus and His glorified saints will put their feet on the head and neck of the Devil and have him bound and cast into the abyss, which will be the bruising referred to by Jehovah at the beginning of human history, and these words in Genesis 3:15 will be literally accomplished.

How wonderful it is that we should have in the third of Genesis a picture of the judgment day, and of the curse upon sin, and of the various degrees and kinds of punishment, all forming an accurate prophecy of what will take place in the winding up of human probation.

12

The Way of Cain

The Apostle Jude mentions three great typical sinners that represent all the various kinds of sinners in the world throughout all generations. He speaks of "the way of Cain," and the "error of Balaam," and the "gainsaying of Korah." If we will search into the conduct of these three great sinners, we will find that the Holy Ghost has selected them as representatives of the three great forms of sin in the world. Cain represents the world, and Balaam represents the flesh, and Korah represents the Devil. In another passage the Holy Spirit classifies their sin in the world under three heads of being earthly, sensual, and devilish. It is impossible for anyone to commit a sin that does not range itself under one of these heads. It was Balaam that managed to seduce the men of Israel with the impure women of Moab, and he stands for all the sins of the flesh. It was Korah that rebelled against Moses and set up an anti-Christ religion among the Israelites, and he stands for the sins of the Devil. It was Cain that went out from the presence of God and attempted to build an earthly paradise for himself without any reference to the future life or to salvation, and he stands for the sins of the world. God picked out three great representative saints in the Old Testament and tells Ezekiel three times that the most righteous men were Noah, Job, and Daniel. As God had His three representative saints, so the Devil had his three representative sinners.

We have in the fourth chapter of Genesis an outline of the sins of Cain and how he developed a character emphatically for this world. When Cain was born his mother Eve thought he was the Messiah, for at his birth she said, "I have gotten a man from the Lord," but the original signifies "I have gotten the Jehovah Man," the God-Man. You see God had promised that her seed should bruise the serpent's head, and she naturally expected that her firstborn would fulfil that promise, and so she fancied that Cain was the God-Man, but he turned out to be a murderer. The word "Cain" means acquisition, to gain, to acquire wealth and power and glory. Now notice the steps in this man's career as a great representative sinner of the world.

1. Of course the first thing is he was born in the image of his father Adam, which was a fallen, sinful nature. Adam begot his son in his own likeness and after his image. It is true that this word applies to Seth, but it just as truly applies to Cain, who was the first-born. The Scripture abundantly proves that all of Adam's race inherited his fallen, sinful nature. Jesus is the only man of the human race that had no corrupt, evil nature in Him, because He did not have a human father, but was conceived by the Holy Ghost and born of the holy virgin. Scripture shows that human depravity comes from Adam more properly than from Eve. It was not the seed of man that should bruise the serpent's head, but the seed of the woman. And this puts an infinite difference between the humanity of Jesus and the humanity of any other man. Hence Cain inherited the moral character of his father, and this birth-sin which he inherited formed the basis or the seed corn out of which came his subsequent life.

2. The next step in the way of Cain was that of rejecting salvation by sacrificial blood and instituting a natural and vegetable religion in the place of accepting salvation by the sacrifice of a substitute. We read that in process of time Cain brought the fruit of the ground as an offering to the Lord. The words "process of time" in the original are "at the end of the days," that is, at the end of the week, on the Sabbath, when the family gathered together for worship. Abel brought a lamb, the fattest and best of his flock, for it is evident that God had taught Adam and Adam had taught his children the way of worship and the offering of sacrifice and all about the significance of the sacrifice and about the prophetic import of a coming Saviour.

Cain deliberately rejected the sacrificial lamb and insisted on presenting to God only the fruit of the ground. He thereby disclaimed any need of a sacrifice for his sins, and set up for himself a religion of nature, without the confession of sins or the need of a Saviour. He depended alone on himself and his own works as a sufficiency for moral character, and thereby arrayed himself against

56

the promised Son of God and the promised Saviour. Thus Cain became the father of all the Unitarians and Christian Scientists and Mormons and Spiritualists and all the anti-Christ cults of religion in the whole world. It was out of this rejection of salvation by the atoning blood that came his envy and jealousy and murder and every other sin of his life. His great sin did not consist in the fact that he was born with a fallen nature, but in the fact that he rejected God's remedy for sin. Jesus emphasized in His teaching that the great sin was in rejecting the remedy that God had provided for sinners.

At the very beginning of human history we see as perfect a setting forth of self-righteousness and rejecting of the atonement and the various developments of sin as can be found in all successive generations. God told Cain that there was a sin offering lying at his door, for the word "sin" in Genesis 4:7 should be "sin offering," and that if Cain would present that sin offering, the sacrificial lamb, he would be accepted, but he despised salvation according to God's plan, and that became the inward cause in his heart of all other forms of sin.

3. In the next place there sprang up envy against Abel because Abel's sacrifice was accepted, and this envy led to murder. The passion of envy has produced more murders than all other passions in the human heart put together. It was envy that sold Joseph, that made Saul persecute David, that made the princes try to kill Daniel, that sold Jesus, and that has been the passion producing murder in all generations.

4. In the next place Cain gave way to despair and said his punishment was greater than he could bear, but the word literally translated is "My sin is too great to be pardoned." That was the language of unbelief, because if he had accepted salvation by the sacrifice of another, he would have found that the sin of murder could be pardoned the same as any other sin. Murder was not the greatest of his sins, but the rejection of God's plan of salvation was even greater than that of murder.

5. In the next place we are told that Cain went out from the presence of God. Here we have the self-righteous, impenitent rejector of the atonement parting company with the living God, and

going out from the divine presence to be forever banished from the favor of God.

6. In the next place we see Cain going eastward and raising a large family and building a city and his children inventing musical instruments. His whole life work consisted in trying to build an earthly paradise of cities and parks and gardens and music and flowers and earthly pleasure, earthly wealth, absolutely ignoring the living God and all of God's plans, having no prayer, no divine revelation, no communication with heaven, no faith in the great things of the future world. He was a man wholly devoted to the pleasures of this present world.

This is what the Holy Ghost calls "the way of Cain." And now just look at it: it all came from a self-righteous spirit that deliberately rejected the atoning blood of the promised seed and undertook to set up a religion of nature in defiance to the revealed religion through the Son of God. There are tens of thousands of men living on earth today who are reproducing every form and feature of the way of Cain, and in all these thousands of years the image of Adam has never improved and never would improve if the world should stand for millions of ages.

13

God's First Cemetery

In the fifth chapter of Genesis we have an account of the death of all the first patriarchs, from Adam to Lamech, and in the last verse we have the mention of Noah and his three sons, thereby giving us in this one chapter the first ten names in the direct succession of the human race. We may style this chapter the Westminster Abbey of the Old Testament or God's First Cemetery, because we have the mention of the lives and deaths of all those men in succession.

The first age or dispensation of the human race extended from Adam to the flood, and at the beginning of that dispensation we have the death of Abel, and just before the close of that dispensation we have the translation of Enoch, forming, as it were, the termini of that age. There are similar things that belong to the present church age or dispensation, for at the beginning of this age we have the death of Christ, and at the close of the age will come the Rapture or the translation of the righteous, who are caught up to meet the Lord in the air. Thus the death of Abel and the death of Christ correspond with each other at the beginning of the age, and the translation of Enoch and the Rapture of the saints correspond at the close of each age. If we search closely enough we will find that every successive age or dispensation of human history has been patterned after the first age, proving in all things God's first words supply the key to all successive words. Now if we study the names that are mentioned in this fifth chapter of Genesis, we find in the significance of those names an unfolding of the successive facts connected with redemption.

1. The name "Adam" signifies a man of the earth, or more literally red earth, which sets forth the doctrine of the Incarnation. As God breathed the breath of life into Adam and he became a living and everlasting soul, so God incarnated the personal and eternal Son

of God into a human body, born of the virgin Mary, and thereby sent into the world the second Man, the second Adam. Thus the way God formed the first man was a picture of the Incarnation which God proposed from eternity.

If we study the remarkable words in Proverbs 8:22-31, we will see that those words refer to the Son of God, and that from eternity there was a plan of divine incarnation in a man, "for His delights were with the sons of men." The words in verse thirty which read, "Then was I as one brought up with Him" should be translated "Then I was by Him as the world builder;" that is, the Son was with the Father as the world builder from the beginning, and this "world builder" was the delight of God the Father. Also it was "His delight to dwell with the sons of men," which explains the motive for the Incarnation. This Incarnation was not a temporary thing to pass away, but is to last throughout all future eternity.

2. The name "Seth" signifies "a substitute," and he was given that name because his mother said he took the place of Abel, who had been slain. This was prophetic of Jesus Christ; that as the second Man He was to be a substitute for sinners, to take the place of Adam the first, and die for the human race. The substitution of Christ for the sinner is one of the strongest doctrines set forth in the Bible, and these higher critics or infidel preachers that represent the death of Christ only as a moral force or as a martyr are a long way from the real Bible teaching. The fact that Jesus died, the just for the unjust, and took the place of a lost sinner on the cross, is abundantly proved by every passage in Scripture referring to that subject. The prophet says that Christ made His soul an offering for sin, which took place in the Garden of Gethsemane. And then the apostle says that He bore our sins in His own body, which took place on the cross. In both cases Christ was the true Seth for the human race, the substitute for the lost.

3. The name "Enos" signifies mortality, or death, and this name was prophetic of the death of Christ. He was not only a substitute, as the word "Seth" signifies, but He must of necessity pay the death penalty for sin, according to the words that eating the forbidden fruit would be punished with death. The sufferings of Christ in

60

themselves could not meet the perfect requirement of the law, but those sufferings must terminate in death, and you will notice in the Scriptures it is always the death of Christ that becomes the procuring cause of our salvation. If Christ had suffered twice as much as He did suffer and then had not died, His sufferings would not have saved us, because the necessity was placed on the fact "that He died," the just for the unjust.

4. The name "Cainan" signifies acquisition, to buy back, to purchase a lost estate, and this is exactly what Christ accomplished by His death. When Christ died, He paid the redemption price sufficient for the saving of every human being, and also sufficient to pay off the mortgage that Adam gave to the Devil upon the earth, and by which He redeemed every single thing that had been lost. Christ paid the sufficient price for saving the race from sin, and for the resurrection of the dead bodies, and for the restoring the earth to its primitive pure condition, and removing all the curse from the lower creation, making ample provision for what the apostle calls "the restitution of all things."

5. The name "Mahalaleel" signifies "the splendor of God," and was prophetic of the glorious resurrection of Christ, by which He emerged from the grave, and from the land of shadows, and appeared in His glorified body, and revealed to His followers the splendor of immortality and everlasting life; and by that glorious resurrection He manifested forth the glory of the resurrection of His saints.

6. The name "Jared" signifies "descending, or pouring out," or coming down as a shower of rain from the clouds, and sets forth in a most beautiful way the descent of the Holy Spirit on the day of Pentecost, coming down from the ascended Saviour. The Holy Spirit existed and operated through all of the past dispensations, from Adam to Pentecost, but after Christ ascended He then sent down the Holy Spirit as the personal Sanctifier and Comforter for His church, and gave the Holy Ghost the authority to possess His people and distribute to them the nine gifts of the Spirit.

7. The name "Enoch" signifies "to teach," to "impart instruction, knowledge, wisdom, and understanding." This name corresponds exactly with the work that Jesus said the Holy Ghost would perform,

that He would teach the disciples and show them things to come and guide them into all truth, and comfort them under all circumstances. Thus the name "Enoch" agrees exactly with the work of the Holy Ghost that He should perform after Pentecost.

We see that Enoch was the seventh from Adam and he did not die. This also was prophetic, that at the beginning of the seventh day of human history, that is, the seventh thousand years, that the people of God would not die, but pass into the Millennial age and be free from death. This corresponds with the seventh day of human history, and the seventh man from Adam.

8. The name "Methuselah" signifies "to be released from death." After Jesus rose from the dead He announced that He had the keys of death and Hades, and the power to translate living saints without dying. He told Peter that if He wanted to do so, He could preserve the Apostle John alive without dying unto His second coming.

9. The name "Lamech" signifies "a conqueror," or an "over-thrower"; that is, one that subdues his enemies, and tears down any opposing kingdom. This name agrees exactly with what Christ will do at His Second Coming, when He will chain Satan and grind in pieces all the kingdoms of the world, and subdue the whole earth, and bring everything in the world under His complete subjection.

10. The name "Noah" signifies "rest," and corresponds exactly with the Millennial Age, which will be the Sabbath Day of the world's history, the day of rest after the six days, or six thousand years of turmoil, strife, and misgovernment.

Now it is certain that these names were not given by chance, but they were used by the Holy Ghost as prophetic of things to come in the age of salvation. Thus the first age furnishes us with the key to unlock the great outlines of salvation in Christ Jesus, from the Incarnation clear through to the time when Christ shall return and reign on the earth and bring the age of peace and rest.

14

The First Prophetic Judgment Day

If we study the account of the flood as recorded in the sixth and seventh chapters of Genesis in connection with the words of Christ in Matthew, that His second coming will be like Noah's flood, we will find an exact setting forth of all the outlines of the judgment day in the record of the flood. I use the words "judgment day" in this connection concerning the judgment of the living nations more particularly and not the judgment of the wicked dead, which will take place after the thousand-year reign of Christ. At the time of the flood there was a transition from the first to the second age or dispensation, and that transition was accompanied with a great many marvelous changes in the material creation, and in the animal system, and in the habits of both man and beast. Let us notice the various items about the flood and see how they correspond with the things that will occur in connection with the coming of the Lord.

1. The people living on the earth had filled up the cup of their iniquity, which was the occasion for the flood. If we notice the words in the sixth of Genesis we see that the human race gave themselves up to all manner of fleshly impurity and fierceness of spirit and pride in every form, so that it became a necessity for God to wash the inhabitants from the surface of the earth and start the human race over again.

There is a ripeness to sin just the same as there is to grain or fruit, and God has taught us in His Word that He waits for sin to reach a certain point of maturity before He sends judgment. He told Abraham that his children could not at that time take possession of the land of Canaan because the iniquity of the Amorites had not yet been filled, showing that God waited for their cup of sin to get full before He ordered their destruction by Joshua.

This same truth will apply to the winding up of the church age and the Second Coming of Jesus. Sin has many forms to take, and the shape of iniquity may not be the same at the winding up of the church age that it was at the winding up of the first age. But the iniquity of this age will reach its climax in an utter rejection of a supernatural Saviour and a supernatural religion and everything will be reduced to material science and human pride and the making a god out of humanity.

2. The ark was most certainly a type of Christ as a Saviour. The Roman Catholics teach that the ark was a type of the Romish church, but how can the church save the church? Noah and his family represent the church that was saved in the ark, and if Noah and his family represent the church, how can the ark represent the church? The whole heresy is based on the notion that the Romish church is a saviour, which is the very spirit of anti-Christ. Just as the ark was manifested as a saviour and Noah and his family went up into the ark, so at the close of this age the Lord Jesus will be manifested from Heaven, and His people will be caught up through the air to meet Him, and they will thereby be rescued from the judgments coming on the earth.

3. It was said in Genesis 7:11 that Noah was six hundred years old when he entered the ark, which corresponds with the fact that the Second Coming of Christ will take place six thousand years after the creation.

4. We read that when Noah and his family entered the ark God shut him in, which is a significant fact that God alone knows who will be the ones that are prepared for translation at the coming of Christ. And God alone will have authority as to who shall be taken and who shall be left, and who they will be that are shut in with Christ in the place of safety up in the heavens.

5. After the door was shut, which is a picture of the Rapture of the saints, then the fountains inside the earth were broken up and the windows of heaven were opened to let down the vast amount of waters that had been kept above the firmament from the creation, and the whole earth was in an upheaval and a letting loose of all the elements. It is evident that at the time of the flood God struck

the earth with a terrible blow and deranged all the ordinary laws of nature, and knocked the earth at that time out of its proper relation to the sun and the north star.

Before the flood we are told that the earth was watered by heavy mists and dews and evidently there was no rain or thunder or lightning or earthquakes or any severe winters or any burning summers or any abnormal process in nature, but at the flood the whole system of our world was knocked out of joint. This accounts for the fact that the North Pole is not in proper range with the north star by several degrees. It also accounts for earthquakes, tornadoes, storms, abnormal winters, and scorching summers. It also accounts for the actinic ray in the sunshine, which produces fermentation, and for all the abnormal things that occur in the natural world. It seems evident to me that before the flood the vast majority of waters now on the earth were held up above the firmament in the form of mist, and that at the flood those waters were let down, making the amount of water on the earth so much larger than that of the dry land.

Now at the Second Coming of Christ the great tribulation will come on, and in the time of that judgment period we are told in several places "God will smite the earth" and "make it stagger like a drunken man," and at that time God will knock the earth back into its normal relation to the sun and the north star; so that in the Millennial Age all the abnormal things that we now have will pass away.

6. We read that the rain fell forty days and forty nights, which I take as a prophetic intimation that the great tribulation will last forty years. Many teach that the tribulation judgment will last only seven years, but that is the length of time for the anti-Christ, but the anti-Christ does not rise until towards the close of the great tribulation. Forty is always the number in Scriptures for judgment. It rained forty days, and Nineveh had forty days to prepare for judgment, and the Israelites were condemned to wander forty years in the wilderness, and Moses, Elijah, and Jesus fasted forty days, and it was forty years from the death of Christ to the destruction of Jerusalem. Hence it would seem that the forty days of rain at the flood is a prophetic type of the forty years of the tribulation judgment.

7. While the nations on the earth were being drowned in the flood, Noah and his family were safely shut in the ark and floated above the waters. This is a picture of the security of those saints who are caught up to meet the Lord in the air and of their being shut in with Christ while the nations on the earth are undergoing the great tribulation. Noah and his family could not see the terrible desolation of the flood, for there was only one window and that was at the top; and so the raptured saints will not see the awful tribulation that takes place on the earth. When the Hebrews crossed the Red Sea they did not see the terrible destruction of the army of Pharaoh that pursued them, because there was a great cloud placed between the Hebrews and the Egyptians. Thus in all these cases the righteous who are rescued from the judgments of God are not allowed to see the awful calamities put on the wicked in the judgment.

8. When the waters subsided the ark rested on a mountain, and this was a prophetic type of Christ returning with His glorified saints after the tribulation judgment and standing on Mount Olivet, and taking possession of the world to start the new dispensation of the kingdom of God, when righteousness shall fill the earth as waters fill the sea.

15

The First Type of the Holy Spirit

In the eighth chapter of Genesis we have an account of Noah
sending forth two birds from the ark, the raven and the dove. The
raven was sent forth first and then the dove. The raven is a type of
Satan, and the dove is a type of the Holy Spirit, but Satan has his
day first and God has His day afterwards. The first time that the
Holy Spirit is mentioned is in the second verse in Genesis, where
we read that the "Spirit of God moved upon the face of the waters."
The word "moved" should more properly be translated "brooded."
And hence the very first time that the Holy Spirit is mentioned in
God's Word He is spoken of as a bird, a dove, with His outstretched
wings brooding over the primeval elements of creation. And in this
account of Noah sending forth the dove we have the same thought
as expressed in the first chapter, that the Holy Ghost is revealed
under the emblem of a dove. When Jesus was baptized the Holy
Ghost descended on Him in the form of a dove. Here we have
three separate manifestations of the Spirit of God acting under the
emblem of a dove, and we see from the beginning to the end that
God's first word is never changed, but that all the operations of the
Holy Ghost in later dispensations correspond with the revelation of
His work in the beginning.

When the raven was sent from the ark it went to and fro over
the waters, but did not return to the ark, which corresponds with the
words of Satan in the book of Job when he told God that "he was
going to and fro in the earth," and also corresponds with the words
of the apostle that Satan is like a roaring lion "going about," restless,
seeking whom he may devour. Jesus is compared to a lamb, and
when the Devil attacks Christ or the saints he is compared to a roaring lion because lions kill lambs. On the other hand the Holy Ghost
is compared to a dove, and when Satan is spoken of as antagonizing

the Holy Ghost he is then compared to a raven, because ravens kill doves. Hence we see the perfect typology in Scripture as referring to Christ or the Holy Spirit or Satan. The dove was sent forth by Noah on a special mission, "to see if the waters were abated from the earth," but nothing is said about the raven being sent forth on any mission. We see that the dove made three visits out across the waters, which are very significant of the ministry of the Spirit in the world and to individuals.

1. The dove found no place for her foot and hence at the close of the day returned to the ark. This sets forth the fact that the Holy Ghost moved across the first dispensation, brooding over the human race, to find, if possible, sufficient place in human hearts to establish a church or a spiritual kingdom where He might lodge with human beings. It is true that in the first dispensation, from Adam to the flood, there were conspicuous cases of individual righteousness and doubtless multitudes served God. But in all those generations the service of God was confined to individuals, and there was no church formed and no law was given and no organized religious movement such as were manifested in later dispensations. The human race waxed worse and worse in sin, until the Holy Spirit left the world and returned again to God and the judgment of the flood was sent to destroy the race.

This also corresponds with the fact that with the individual sinner the Holy Ghost broods over him and seeks to find a place for His foot in the human soul. But when the sinner persists in a life of wickedness and impenitence the heavenly Dove leaves him and returns to God. So that the first visit of Noah's dove out over the waters, without finding a place for her foot, is significant both of the moral condition of the first age of the race, and also of the condition of the impenitent sinner.

2. In the second visit that the dove made she found an olive leaf on the side of some mountain, and plucked it off and took it back to Noah in the ark. This is a prophetic type of the visit that the Holy Ghost made to the world in the Mosaic age, for in that dispensation He found some signs of the kingdom of God and signs of a new life coming into the world sufficient to furnish the olive leaf for Him to

pluck off. In the Jewish age there was established the giving of the law, the formation of the kingdom of Israel, the sacrificial types and prophecies concerning Christ and the raising up of great prophets and priests and holy men, indicating the formation of a new religious movement among men, corresponding with the olive leaf that appeared on the mountain side at the subsidence of the flood. It is evident that the flood occurred in the spring of the year, probably the first week in April, and the dove was looking for something to build her nest with, that she might lay her eggs and raise her young. Thus we may regard the Jewish dispensation as the springing up of a new life in the human race by the giving of the law and the institution of a divine religion among men.

This second visit of the dove also corresponds with the Spirit brooding over the true penitent and bringing a new life into the soul, corresponding with the olive branch of pardon and peace. It is always springtime when a soul is converted in that individual's life. Thus the Holy Spirit finds in the young convert the dawning of a new life, of a new year, but still the condition of the soul is not so thoroughly renewed as to furnish a permanent place for the heavenly Dove.

3. The third time that the dove went forth from the ark she found the ground sufficiently dry to build her nest and remain there, and hence did not return to the ark any more. We must remember that doves do not build their nests in trees, but on the ground, and this dove was looking for a place on the ground sufficiently dry to build her nest. This corresponds with the fact that after Christ died and rose again and gathered His disciples in the upper room, the Holy Ghost was sent upon them. There was in the hearts of at least one hundred and twenty of the disciples a condition sufficient to receive the Holy Ghost to abide with them and make His home in the hearts of the saints. Hence the Holy Ghost, the heavenly Dove, when He came to the earth at Pentecost came to abide with the church through all the dispensation down to the time of the Rapture, and this abiding of the Spirit in the world throughout the Gospel age corresponds with the third visit of Noah's dove, when she

found a place to lay her eggs and raise her young and did not return to Noah anymore.

This also agrees with the fact that when the believer is fully given up to Christ and receives Him as a perfect Savior, he is in a condition to receive the Holy Spirit as the abiding Comforter, to remain in him and with him forever. Just as Noah's dove, after building her nest, reproduced herself by raising her young, so the holy Spirit, when He finds an abiding place in the heart of the perfect believer, will reproduce the life of Christ in that soul. Just as the Holy Spirit produced the Incarnation of the Lord Jesus and wrought out the will of God in the life of Christ, so He has been sent down from the ascended Savior to enter our hearts and form Christ within us, the hope of glory, and repeat over again in a most marvelous way the life of the blessed Jesus, and prepare us for our ascension at the coming of the Lord just as He prepared Jesus for His ascension to the right hand of God the Father.

Now only think of it, the first time that the Holy Spirit is mentioned in the Bible He is set forth as a dove, brooding over the dark elements of primeval creation, and forming the elements into a world of harmony and beauty and order, for Isaiah says that it is by the Holy Spirit that "the heavens are garnished," and that first picture of the work of the Holy Ghost goes right on through all creation and redemption and the various dispensations of human history without any change in the significance of His work.

16

The First Four Typical Men

Have you ever thought of the great significance of the four men that were preserved in the ark at the time of the flood? The number four is always that special number in Scripture that refers to the earth or the human race. Each number in the Bible has a special significance of its own. As the number two always refers to covenants, testimony, and witnessing, and the number three always refers in some way to God, the three Divine Persons, so the number four always refers in some way to the human or the world or things relating to the destiny of mankind. Not only were those four men in the ark significant of God's purpose and plan in connection with redemption, but in every instance where the four men are referred to there is always one major and three minors. We see that Noah was the major member and his three sons were the minor members in that illustrious and prophetic quartet. In the book of Daniel we have an account of the three Hebrew children in the fiery furnace, and there appeared in visible form the Son of God, making four, but the Son of God was the major member and the three Hebrews were the minor members in that wonderful company. At the transfiguration we see another setting forth of this illustration of four. Here Jesus was the major member and Peter, James, and John were the minor members of that illustrious company.

In the second chapter of Numbers God gave to Moses a plan for the formation of the twelve tribes into four armies, three tribes to each army. The formation of those armies is significant of things connected with the kingdom of God from the beginning to the end. There were on the east side of the camp, toward the sun rising, the three tribes of Judah, Issachar, and Zebulun, with the picture of a lion on their banners. On the south side were stationed the tribes of Reuben, Simeon, and Gad, with the picture of an ox on their banners. On the west were stationed the three tribes of Ephraim, Manasseh, and Benjamin, with a man on their banners. On the north were stationed the three tribes of Dan, Asher, and Naphtali, with a flying eagle on their banners. Here we see four armies, and the law holds good that on one banner was the face of a man, the major member, and on the other three the pictures of the lion, the ox, and the eagle, who were the minor members. These four armies corresponded exactly with the four men in Noah's ark, and the four men in the fiery furnace, and the four men at the transfiguration.

In the next place, we find that this number four agrees exactly with the four Gospels. Matthew gives us the life of Christ as a king, corresponding to the lion. Mark gives us the life of Christ as a servant, corresponding to the ox. Luke gives us the life of Christ in His full humanity, corresponding to the man. John gives us the life of Christ especially in His deity, corresponding to the flying eagle. It is Luke that mentions more things about the humanity of Christ than all the other Gospels, and it is John that mentions more about the deity of Jesus than all the other Gospels.

These instances of a four-fold representation are carried throughout the Old Testament and the New Testament, and unto the Second Coming of the Lord and the Rapture of the church, and the things portrayed in the judgment day in the book of Revelation. The four living creatures mentioned in Revelation agree in every point with this four-fold representation, from Noah's ark clear through the Bible. We should never read "the four beasts," for the original word signifies "the four living ones." The word there translated "beast" in the four living creatures is the same word in the original where Christ says, "I give unto you eternal life," and how absurd would it be to read the words "I give unto you eternal beast;" hence the word should always be read "the four living ones." But when the word "beast" is used in Revelation 13 about the anti-Christ, there the Greek word is "therion," which always means a wild, ferocious beast.

The four living creatures mentioned in Revelation are not angels, but redeemed men. It says in chapter 5 that they had been redeemed by the blood of Christ from all nations and tongues and people, proving that they are a company of saints that stand the very highest in the kingdom of God. They represent a large number who have been gathered out from the saved ones of the earth and put in the front rank of the saints of God.

God tells us in Ezekiel, in three places, that Noah, Job, and Daniel were the most righteous men in the Old Testament, and Jesus puts John the Baptist up in the same rank. So here we have that wonderful number four, representatives of the great saints of God, of which John the Baptist was the major member and Noah, Job, and Daniel were the minor members of that wonderful company.

Another significant fact is that in the book of Revelation, every time that the four living creatures are referred to as performing any action, it is always something in relation to the earth, but when the twenty-four elders are referred to as performing any action, it is always in relation to things in Heaven. This proves that the number four always refers to things belonging to the earth or to the human race.

This is not all, but in matters connected with the Bride of Christ the number four is very significant. In the forty-fifth Psalm David gives us a picture of Jesus and His Bride, for the first half of the Psalm is a picture of the Bridegroom, and the second half is a picture of the Bride. Now in connection with the bridal company, the Psalmist mentions the queen, the bride dressed in the gold of Ophir, and then he mentions three other companies of saved ones. He speaks of the daughter of Tyre, which represents a company saved from the ancient Gentiles, and then another company spoken of as honorable women, and then the fourth company spoken of as the virgins. Here we have four distinct companies referred to that are saved from the earth, but the queen, the Bride of Christ, is the major member, and the other three are the minor members.

The same truth is referred to in the Song of Solomon, sixth chapter, where the prophet speaks of three score queens, who are a company of saved ones, and fourscore concubines, who represent another company of saved ones, and the virgins without number, who represent another company of saved ones. But over and above all these there is mentioned "My dove, my undefiled," who is the elect one of her mother, the chosen one of all. Here we see that the elect one of all is the queen, the Bride of the Lamb, the major member. And then the other three companies are the minor members.

The same truth is brought out again in Revelation 22:17, in regard to sending forth invitations for human beings to drink freely of the water of life. We see there are four invitations. The first is from the Bride of Christ, who stands next to the Holy Spirit. The Bride says "Come," and then in the second place, "Let him that heareth say, Come," and then in the third place, "Let him that is athirst come," and then in the fourth place, "Let whosoever will come and take the water of life." Here there are four invitations, but the Bride is the major member, and the three others are the minor members in the company.

It would be absolutely absurd to say or to suppose that all these things could happen by chance in the Bible. No; they are all divinely inspired, and all refer to one and the same great subject. They are all connected with redemption, with God's plan of salvation among men, and set forth the various ranks in the coming kingdom of the Lord Jesus Christ. All these things are set forth in a prophetic form by the four men that were saved in Noah's ark.

Here we see that God's first words relating to those four men in the ark go straight forward down through all Scripture and all various dispensations, and come out in the end of the Bible and in the end of redemption in a vast significance, setting forth the kingdom of the Lord Jesus Christ in relation to the human race.

17

The First Babylon

Babylon existed in the heart and mind of the backslidden children of Noah before it ever existed in the form of a city or a tower. Babylon has its root in a rebellious mind, and takes its form in the imagination of a proud, self-conceited soul, and afterwards is formulated in an open revolt against God and an organized effort to outwit the Almighty.

We have in Genesis 11 the account of the first building of Babylon. A thousand years after this there was another Babylon built by the great Nebuchadnezzar, who conquered the whole world at the time that the Jews were led into captivity. At the winding up of this age, and in connection with the second coming of Christ, there is the ultimate Babylon in mystery, described in Revelation, which will be the climax of all the Babylons, and is to go down in everlasting destruction. Everything that is mentioned in the Bible in connection with Babylon has its seed corn in the record of this chapter, and here we have a sample record of every trait connected with Babylon, and also a sample of God's final judgment on the pride and sin that originated this Babylon. In connection with this original Babylon, please note the following points:

1. After the decline of the posterity of Noah from the true service of God, it is said that the men journeyed eastward, until they found the plain of Shinar, by the river Euphrates. It is also said that Cain went eastward. God's pilgrims go west, but Satan's children migrate to the east. The children of Jacob went west, but the children of Esau went east. Abraham went west, and the apostles, at the beginning of the Gospel, went west. There is something very significant in these historical facts, that down through all the centuries God's movements go with the sun and travel west, and Satan's movements go against the sun and go east. At the second coming of

Jesus, He tells us He will come like a flash of lightning out from the east and go toward the west. He will appear in the sky over Bethlehem, where He was born, and travel in the air westward around the earth, and raise the righteous dead and gather up the righteous living to Himself in the air, until He encircles the globe. Do you see that the first things in history always furnish the key to successive events, clear down to the end of human history?

2. The next item in this account is that of fallen, depraved men who had revolted from the God of their father Noah, forming themselves into a human association. They said, "Go to, let us build a city." In this human association there was no mention of the name of God, but the whole plan was a product of the pride and vanity of heart depravity. From that day until this, human history has been filled with all sorts of human associations and oath-bound societies and confederations of men in every form of compact, and for every conceivable purpose. And the great world-wide oath-bound associations which will reach their climax in the days of the anti-Christ will be but the perfect heading up and consummation of this wretched confederation of a human association which instituted the beginning of Babylon. God has never formed but two organizations in this world apart from the family, and they were Israel and the Christian Church. Israel was God's formation for Himself of a society in the Old Testament, and the Church is the formation of His society in the New Testament. These are the only two associations that God has organized in the history of the world, and both of these were formed for His Son.

3. Notice the items that those rebellious sinners mentioned when they said, "Let us build us a city and a tower and a name." The city was the largest, and in the city was to be a tower rising so high that God could not drown it with another flood. On the top of the tower they were to put their name, which was to be the climax of the whole rebellious ambition. Here we see the different steps of ambition, and how it climbs up from the surface of the earth to a point somewhere in the sky, that purposes to usurp the place of God and take the place of the name of God. The whole structure was built on the earth, and for the earth, and like the earth, without any reference

to God, without the mention of His name, but a vast scheme of boundless vanity. It was to be anti-God, anti-Christ, and to be the consummation of everything that was in fallen human nature.

In all this we see the beginning of that movement in human history which will reach its climax in the days of the anti-Christ, and which is now moving forward at a rapid pace in the various oath-bound labor unions and other associations which utterly ignore the God of the Bible and the Lord Jesus Christ.

4. Notice the material that they would use in the structure of the city and the tower—namely, brick and slime. Where Babel was built in the land of Shinar, there were no rocks, but a plain of rich, loamy soil which could easily be made into brick. In all Scripture the brick is a symbol of a human formation and of a material opposed to God. The Lord prohibited the Jews from making anything out of brick, for they were to build of stone. The Jewish altar was to be constructed of rock, without being polished or having any tool used upon it. We see in Isaiah 65:3 that God condemned the backslidden Israelites for building altars of brick, as was the custom of the heathen. These sinners of Babel had no lime, and so they used slime or mud as plaster to cement the bricks together with. Slime or mud is a symbol of human policy as opposed to the straightforwardness of perfect veracity and truth between man and man. The apostle tells us that the living stones in God's structure are cemented together with love, and believers are to be knit fast to each other in love. But, on the other hand, we notice in Scripture that all sinful associations of men are held together by selfish interests, by policy, by mere human sentiment and a spirit of time-serving and treachery and deceit, which is all expressed by the use of slime instead of plaster.

5. We notice God's judgment on this vain enterprise of human pride. God came down and put a curse upon them in smiting their vocal organs, or confounding their mental perception in the use of words, and divided their speech so that they could not understand each other, and thus had to quit building the tower. Here we see God's first judgment on Babylon, from which the name is taken, for the word signifies confusion, misunderstanding, which leads to division and strife.

At Pentecost the Holy Ghost caused the disciples to speak in seventeen different languages so that the people gathered to Jerusalem from the various nations could hear in their own speech of the wonderful works of God in their souls, and that miracle at Pentecost was counterpart to this miracle in the dividing of tongues at Babel. In the first instance it was a miracle of dividing the speech and leading to division and separation, but at Pentecost it was a miracle of bringing together the different nations and languages of the earth to hear the Gospel.

In the coming age, when Jesus reigns on the earth, we are told in Zephaniah 3:9 that the world will all speak one pure language. Hence after the great Babylon in mystery is utterly destroyed, as in Revelation 18, and when Christ reigns, as in Revelation 20, the last trace of Babylon will pass away from the earth. There will be no more any division of speech, or any misunderstanding among the people who live in that blessed age.

6. We notice the name of Nimrod in connection with the building of Babel, (Genesis 10:10). It is evident that Nimrod founded a kingdom for himself, and the whole aim was to make his great city the headquarters for all backsliders in the world who had revolted against the religion taught by Noah. The Scriptures mention four distinct countries in relation to moral character. Egypt is always the land of sin and for sinners. The wilderness is always the country of the imperfect believer, those who are not established in the faith, but who are going about to establish their own righteousness. Canaan is always the land of the perfect believer, the victorious servant of God, the inheritance of the fulness of blessing, the typical country for the abiding Comforter and the exploits of the believer in the power of the Holy Ghost. Babylon is always the land of backsliders, the country for those who have fallen into sin and turned away from the true faith. If you will study these four countries in every place where they are mentioned in the Bible, you will find that in every instance these countries stand for the character that I have mentioned.

Thus all the Babylons that are mentioned, from the tower of Babel down to the judgment on Babylon in mystery in Revelation, always stand for apostasy, and the doom that comes on Babylon is the doom of the apostate. Thus in this case, as in all others, God's first words persist in their significance and go straightforward through all history down to the end.

18

The First Pilgrim of Faith

As we approach the study of the life of Abraham and the marvelous teaching of his life, we will find that in him there is given us a sample of the first words of God in connection with a great many subjects. These include, for instance, God's first words concerning the pilgrimage of faith, justification by faith, sanctification, complete sacrifice of self, and also concerning the resurrection of the dead, and the everlasting home of the glorified saints in the "city which hath foundations, whose builder and maker is God." In studying the significance of the great characters in the Bible, we find that each one is a whole world in itself of significance and typology, but the teaching in the life of Abraham has a majesty and sweep and extent of import which, taken in the whole from beginning to end, is not surpassed by any character that has ever lived in the world.

The Scriptures mention in a very special way the faith of Abel and Enoch and Noah, but in the case of Abraham we have the first instance of a pilgrimage of faith, the beginning and the on going in the steps of faith, set forth in a life journey from beginning to end. It is this life journey of faith that makes Abraham such an example for the true believer. The Apostle Paul mentions this fact in a special way in Romans, that a true believer who is to share the inheritance of this earth in the coming age must be one that walks in the steps of the faith of Abraham. The words "the steps of faith" set forth the fact that we are on a journey, that we are pilgrims and strangers in the earth in our present life. And if we walk in the steps of Abraham's faith, it will be well for us to notice those steps.

1. Abraham was called to go out from one country into another country. "The Lord said unto Abram, Get thee out of thy country, and from thy kindred, and from thy father's house, unto a land that I will show thee." These are the key words that God speaks to

everyone who is called to follow Christ in a life of faith. There has to be a separation from the old life in order that there may be an entrance upon a new life. There is always the negative and the positive, the coming out from in order to the entering into.

Do you notice the three-fold separation, first from his country, which was a large place, and then from his kindred, who were more limited, and then from his father's house, that is, from the very home in which he had lived. This three-fold separation shows us the perfect giving up of everything of our natural lives in order that we may go with the Lord into His land and His life and His promises, and finally into His glory. Every step in this three-fold separation was getting closer and closer to the individual life and heart of Abram. This three-fold separation was to be followed by the revelation to him of another land and another people and another house that should be his forever. There was not only the giving up of everything he had in life, but in connection with this there was presented something more attractive and more favorable and more lasting to take place of what he had to give up, for there was promised a land that the Lord would show him. He was giving up man's country for God's country, the human life for the divine life, the earthly inheritance for a future and everlasting inheritance. And this is exactly the lesson that God presents to everyone that is called to follow Jesus in a life of true faith.

2. We notice some things that hindered Abram in making this journey of faith. When he left his country in Ur of the Chaldees he took with him his father Terah and his nephew Lot. There is no mention that God ever called Terah and Lot to go with Abram, but they were so closely allied to Abram that it seemed impossible to him at that time to separate himself from them, and so we notice that they journey with Abram toward Canaan until they came to Haran, and there Abram stopped for a while. We do not know how long he lingered there, but it says he remained there until his father Terah died, and then he resumed his journey toward Canaan. How significant this is, and we must remember that it is all a part of God's infallible Word. It has always been true that the old man hinders real progress to Canaan, and Abram did not enter the land promised

to him until after the old man died; and that remains true with the pilgrim of faith all through the generations. We learn elsewhere that Terah worshipped idols, and while he believed in the true God and doubtless was saved in the end, yet his faith was of a very mixed character, and he stands as a monument to that mixed condition of faith which believes in God and yet is swayed by earthly things and a species of idolatry. Lot still journeyed with Abram toward Canaan, but we shall see later on that Lot himself was a hindrance to Abram in his onward progress to carry out the purpose of the Lord in him.

3. We notice that when Abram reached the land of Canaan he passed through the land to Sichem, and took a survey of the country that God promised to him. It was after he entered the land that the Lord appeared unto him and said, "Unto thy seed will I give this land." At that time the Canaanites lived in the land, and when they saw Abram journeying through the country they had no imagination that that majestic, quiet, straightforward man was taking a survey of the country with a prophetic trend and vision in prospect, that all their beautiful country would one day belong to the children of this stranger from the East. In that journey of Abram through Canaan he traversed the beautiful section of Samaria, and then down past Jerusalem, and down through Beersheba, surveying all the beautiful prospects in the very heart of Canaan, and doubtless his faith stretched itself not only over all that land, but also out over the promises of God and unto the destiny of his posterity in the ages to come.

This journey of Abram through Canaan when he surveyed the land is a part of the life of every true believer as he goes forward in the steps of Abram's faith, following Christ toward the inheritance which is to come in the resurrection of the just. How significant it is that every true life of faith must at first take a survey of the promises before they become realized in the living experiences. Faith, in the very nature of things, must be surveyor and navigator and forerunner and discoverer, to spy out possibilities before they become actualities in living fact. As in the case of the man with the measuring line in his hand in Ezekiel's vision, faith must go forward and make the various measurements of a thousand cubits before the soul passes through the waters and actually possesses the experiences of the ankle deep, the knee deep, and the loin deep in the river of the spiritual life.

Abram is the first character mentioned in the Bible as being the surveyor of prospective fields of inheritance. He is held forth as an example of the true believer in studying the promises and surveying God's plan for us, in order to draw us on, that we may make the pilgrimage without faltering clear down to the end.

4. There is much significance in the use of two words in connection with this survey of the land of promise. We first read, "The Lord said unto Abram, Get thee out of thy country," and then in verse seven we read that the Lord appeared unto Abram and said, "Unto thy seed will I give this land." In the first place "God said," but in the second place "the Lord appeared." In the first instance there was a word spoken to Abram's inner sense, or the inner ear of his mind, which he knew most surely was the voice of God, but in the next place there was a divine form that appeared to him, which evidently was not less than the pre-incarnate form of the Son of God, and thus giving him a vision of a Divine Person. So here we see the double manifestation of Jehovah to Abram, first in a word, and then in a living Divine form of a person.

Now this exactly agrees with the true pilgrim of faith in his life journey, for always there is first the promise to the heart, and then the manifestation by the Divine Spirit. How significant are the words of Jesus to Martha and Mary, that if they would believe they should see. "Said I not unto thee, that, if thou wouldest believe thou shouldest see the glory of God?" It is always believe first and see afterward. Here we have this great truth mentioned for the first time in the life of Abram, that there must come in the life of faith first the promise, and then the revelation. God spoke to Eve the promise about her seed, and God gave to Mary the visible manifestation of the blessed person of that promised seed. We are now living the life of faith, but when Christ returns we shall see Him as He is, and be glorified like unto Himself. Those who refuse to believe never get the open vision. It is perfect faith in the spoken promise that prepares the soul for the open vision of the blessed Persons.

5. At the end of that first journey we notice that Abram built an altar, and pitched a tent (Gen. 12:7, 8). Here are two significant facts concerning the pilgrimage of faith, for the building of the altar indicates everything connected with worship and trust in a coming Redeemer, and the need of being saved by a Divine Saviour. Then the pitching of a tent indicates everything in connection with a pilgrimage, for the tent is suggestive of a brief sojourn, with a view of going on to some other place. Abraham never built a city, and so far as we can learn, he never built a house, but lived in a tent. This was not accidental, but a part of God's plan in using him as a picture of the pilgrimage of faith, and as a type of all believers that should come after him; that in our present condition we are pilgrims and strangers going onward, looking for "a city which hath foundations, whose builder and maker is God." This record was not put in the Bible for the sake of Abraham, for he had been gathered to his fathers hundreds of years before this record was made; but it was put down in Holy Scripture for our sakes who are living in this Gospel age.

19

Solar and Lunar Saints

In the 13th chapter of Genesis we have described for the first time in the Bible the difference between solar and lunar saints, which forms the patterns of all subsequent Scriptures bearing on that subject, and showing the different ranks among those who are saved. Abraham was the solar saint, and he dealt directly with God, receiving revelations from God and the communication of the Word of God immediately into his mind, and walking and talking with the infinite Jehovah without an intervening cloud or shadow or human agent. On the other hand, Lot was a lunar saint, who did not deal immediately with God, but obtained his light and knowledge from Abraham. Abraham gazed, as it were, into the face of Jehovah, which Lot did not do, but he received the light of God as it was sifted through the magnificent soul of Abraham and fell upon him in a secondary measure. God spoke directly to Abraham, but did not speak immediately to Lot, but Lot caught the echo of the word of God as it reverberated back to him from the deep canyons of the great man of faith. The different degrees of character between Abraham and Lot as revealed in this chapter, and the different degrees of their faith and of their conduct is a perfect photograph of the first rank and second rank believers which is ever afterwards revealed in Scripture clear down to the end of the Bible. In studying these first words on the different ranks among believers, please notice the following points:

1. Here we have for the first time the complete separation of Abraham from all mixture, not only with the world, but also with weak or half believers. When Abraham left Ur there were two weights hanging upon him. The first was his old father, who died in Haran and left him free to go straight on to Canaan. But now in this chapter we see Abraham separated from the weak believer Lot,

which left him perfectly free to move onward in a sublime journey of boundless faith to the end of his life.

The life of perfect faith, according to Scripture, must be a life of complete separation, not only a separation from the world and from sinners, but a separation in heart and spirit from weak believers, from those who will only go a part of the way in the things of God. There was one separation at Haran, and another separation in the land of Canaan. The Apostle Paul mentions this kind of separation where he says that in a great house there are a great many vessels, not only of gold and silver, but also stone and wood, and if we want God's best we must be separated from these lower vessels. That great house is the Christian church as it exists in the world, and those lower vessels are the weak and carnal Christians who walk largely in the flesh. If anyone wishes to live a victorious life, a life of complete devotion like Abraham, he must be separated from the carnal and Lot-like believers.

2. The occasion for this separation was a dispute between the servants of Abraham and Lot concerning pasture lands for the cattle. That outward circumstance was only an incident that furnished a proper occasion for separation. There existed in the souls of Abraham and Lot two distinct forms of religious life, two distinct standards of life, two distinct degrees of faith, and this outward circumstance of dispute about pasture lands only furnished an opportunity for the moral qualities in these two men to be manifested. This is always so in human character throughout all the generations, that certain qualities exist in the heart, and all that is needed is a proper outward circumstance to give the opportunity for those qualities to manifest themselves. True faith will always manifest its perfect character when the occasion requires it; and, on the other hand, selfishness and unbelief will always manifest themselves under certain conditions.

3. We see the perfect, unselfish faith in Abraham when he gave Lot, his nephew, his own choice. Although Abraham was much older and his uncle and had the prior claim from a natural standpoint, yet he resigned all his rights and all his claim to Lot and said, "You may choose in any direction you please and I will take what is left." Long before this Abraham had chosen God to be his portion,

and he had left his entire life in the hands of the Lord, to go in any direction, to stay anywhere, to take any portion that the Lord might choose for him, and having made the infinite God the choice of his soul and his portion forever, he had no selfish motive in choosing any special locality in the world. Here we see the life of pure faith in choosing God to be our all and in all, and leaving the details of life and fortune in the will of God.

4. We notice in Lot's choice a perfect exhibition of that mixture of faith and doubt, of religion and selfishness, which runs through all generations among those religious people who are mixed in their heart and have the heavenly and the earthly mingled in one life. We read that "Lot lifted up his eyes, and beheld all the Plain of Jordan, that it was well watered everywhere, even as the garden of the Lord. Then Lot chose him all the Plain of Jordan; and Lot journeyed east" and pitched his tent toward Sodom. Every word here reveals an inward character, that in spite of faith in God, the conduct is molded by selfishness. The New Testament affirms that Lot was a righteous man and the Scriptures prove that he was saved, but the Bible never uses the words in connection with Lot that are used in relation to Abraham. God never said to Lot, "Walk before me and be thou perfect," and it is never mentioned that Lot built an altar, and his name is not mentioned as one of the heroes of faith. Every act of a man's life is but the outward blossoming of some secret principle in the heart.

Just notice the three words describing Lot's action. First, he lifted his eyes, and second, he chose the fat pasture, and third, he pitched his tent toward Sodom. These are the three steps of selfishness even though they may be religious. He lifted his eyes to survey the country without any command of God, and then chose the fat lands from a selfish motive, and then he pitched his tent towards Sodom out of sheer weakness, by a sort of earthly gravitation. Those three words are just as true of weak and carnal Christians today as they were in the days of Lot, for every phase of human character persists straight onward through all the generations.

5. Now look at Abraham and watch the action of his soul under the guidance of perfect faith. It says that when Lot was separated

from Abraham, then the Lord spoke to Abram and said, "Lift up now thine eyes, and look from the place where thou art northward and southward, and eastward, and westward: For all the land which thou seest, to thee will I give it, and to thy seed for ever. And I will make thy seed as the dust of the earth." It was when Abram was separated from Lot, his last earthly entanglement, that the Lord spoke to Abram about lifting up his eyes. This is exactly so in the souls of men down to the present hour. It is when we have cut loose from the last entanglement, the last burden of the flesh, and entered into a state of freedom from all earthly burdens that we are in a condition for God to speak to us and open to our vision His promises and His blessing, and His plan.

The Lord said to Abram, "Lift up now thine eyes." Notice the contrast between the two ways of lifting up the eyes, for Lot lifted his eyes in self-will, but Abram lifted his eyes at the command of God. Lot looked in only one direction, and that was east; but Abram was commanded to look in four directions. The place where they were standing was between Mt. Hebron and what is now the Dead Sea, and from those foothills Abram could see as far north as Mt. Lebanon, and as far east as Moab and Mt. Nebo, and as far south as Beersheba, and as far west as the hills that fringed the Mediterranean Sea, giving him a magnificent survey of what was at that time the richest country in the world. There is an infinite difference between the selfish lifting up of the eyes and hunting for our own advantage, and the unselfish lifting up of the eyes at the command of God, with an eye single to His glory, and looking out for those things which pertain to the Kingdom of God and the glory of His Son.

A sample of the difference between the solar and the lunar saints is furnished by St. Paul in his Epistle to the Corinthians, in which he speaks of believers who were really Christians, and they were babes in Christ, but who were lunar saints. They attached their faith to stronger saints instead of laying hold of the fulness of Christ. Some said, "I am of Paul," and others said, "I am of Peter," or "I am of Apollos;" showing that, like Lot, they derived their religious motives and forces more from the great apostles than they did from direct fellowship with the Lord Jesus. Those two classes of Christians mentioned by St. Paul correspond exactly with Abraham and Lot, as recorded two thousand years before the Christian church was formed.

6. In connection with Abraham's unselfish faith in looking to God alone, notice the great promise concerning His seed. The Lord said to Abram, "I will give all the land that thou seest to thy seed, and I will make thy seed like the dust of the earth: so that if a man can number the dust of the earth, then shall thy seed also be numbered." This promise refers especially to the land of Canaan, and it was to be given to Abraham's seed according to the flesh, and that is why the word "dust" is used to illustrate the multitude of Abraham's fleshly posterity. We shall see later on that God gave Abraham another promise referring to his spiritual seed, and speaks of them as being like the stars of heaven. The "dust" seed were to inherit the land which was dust, but later on the "star" seed were to inherit the things of the Kingdom of Heaven. God never promised any blessing to the seed of Lot, because lunar Christians barely get saved themselves, without having spiritual power to bring forth spiritual children to perpetuate their faith.

20

The First Words on Priesthood

The first words in the Bible concerning priesthood are given in the 14th chapter of Genesis in connection with Melchizedek. When Abram returned from the slaughter of the kings, in which he recaptured the people of Sodom, including Lot and his family, there met him Melchizedek, the king of Salem, who brought forth bread and wine, and he was priest of the most high God. He blessed Abram, and said, "Blessed be Abram of the most high God, possessor of heaven and earth," and Abram gave Melchizedek tithes of all the spoils (Gen. 14:17-20). This incident occurred five hundred years before the institution of the Jewish priesthood in the family of Levi, and shows how that the Gentile priesthood was exercised many centuries before the Jewish priesthood, giving the priority to the Gentiles, and not to the Jews. This is worthy of our study.

Paul makes an argument that justification by faith occurred in the life of Abram before the institution of the Jewish system and before circumcision, by which he proves that justification by faith was not a Jewish doctrine, but a Gentile doctrine, and has priority over everything that is Jewish. The same thing is true concerning the priesthood. Now in connection with this Paul tells us that Jesus was made a priest after the order or rank of Melchizedek. He says that if Christ were on the earth He would not be a priest, because He was not of the tribe of Levi, but that being resurrected and ascended at the right hand of God, He is now a priest according to the rank of Melchizedek.

Now you see that the Gentile priesthood existed five hundred years before the Jewish priesthood did, and since the resurrection of Christ the Gentile priesthood has been restored, so that the Jewish priesthood was a parenthesis, coming in between the days of Abraham on the one side and the resurrection of Christ on the other. Hence everything that was peculiar in the Jewish priesthood has been done away, and the only priesthood that exists now is that which existed before the Jewish system was started. So we have the coming together of the first and the last priesthood, both being of the same order or rank.

In the next place, let us notice this man Melchizedek, who was king of Salem and priest of the most high God. You notice he was both a king and a priest, which could not apply to the Jewish economy. He was king of a city on the earth, but he was priest of God, who was in Heaven. This man was greater than Abraham, because Abraham paid tithes to him, and also he had authority from God to put a blessing on Abraham, and Paul says the less is blessed by the greater.

After many years of study I am compelled to discard the old notion that the commentators hold about Melchizedek, and I do not see any way to get around taking the words of Paul in Hebrews as meaning literally what they say. He says that Melchizedek was without father and without mother and without descent or pedigree from any other race of beings, and without beginning or infancy of days, and that he never died, but lived on without dying. Commentators have tried to get around these words in all sorts of ways by making them refer only to the character of his priesthood, but I do not see how it is possible to avoid taking these words just as they read. Jesus, in speaking of John the Baptist, says that of men that were born of women there had never been a greater than John the Baptist, and Jesus, in the use of these words, intimates that there are men, or have been men, that were not born of women. We know that Adam was not born of a woman, and when the apostle tells us that Melchizedek had no father and no mother, I believe the words mean exactly what they say, and that Melchizedek was a man created and put into this world as a special minister of God in the time in which Abraham lived. Nimrod had started a great kingdom in the building of Babylon, which became the headquarters of the apostates after Noah's flood, and it would seem that God created Melchizedek and put him in this world in the west to start a religious movement in opposition to Babylon in the east.

It would seem that Melchizedek built the original city of Jerusalem, and many scholars believe that he may have built the great pyramid in Egypt, which is evidently of supernatural structure. In commenting on Melchizedek, the apostle says he was first the king of righteousness, and afterwards the king of peace. The word "Jerusalem" is made of two words, and the term "Jeru" signifies a foundation of righteousness, and the word "Salem" signifies peace. Those two words are joined together all through Scripture, "righteousness" and "peace," indicative of the fulness of salvation, including forgiveness and purification, and showing that the true inhabitants of Jerusalem are those who are not only justified, but purified. They possess that compound character referred to so many times in Scripture as where we are told that the garments of those in the New Jerusalem consisted of fine linen, pure and radiant, and that the fine linen is the righteousnesses of the saints, for the word "righteous" is in the plural number.

Another point worth knowing is that Melchizedek gave to Abraham a new name for God, which Abraham had never heard before, and which, up to this chapter, was never used in the Scripture, and that is the term "most high God." This name, "most high God," does not occur in the Bible until in this chapter, and the name signifies the God over all the universe, over all worlds and all ages and all orders and ranks of creatures. Abraham believed that God was the supreme One of the universe before this, but he did not use this expression. Melchizedek said, "Blessed be Abram of the most high God," but in a previous verse it is said he was "priest of the most high God." Then when Abram spoke to the king of Sodom he used this new name of God for the first time. He said "he had lifted his hand to the most high God, the possessor of heaven and earth," that he would not take a thread of the spoils for himself, but let the king of Sodom take all. As we journey through this marvelous book of Genesis, and gather out God's first words, we see here another name for the great Jehovah which had not been previously used. It gives us a little larger vision of the character and glory of God.

Let us in conclusion notice the contrast between Jerusalem, where Melchizedek was king, and the city of Babylon, where Nimrod was king. The one was the city of God's peace, the other the city of apostasy and confusion and misunderstanding.

Jerusalem was built in the west, and Babylon in the east. Jerusalem was built on a mountain three thousand feet above the sea, but Babylon was built on a plain almost level with the ocean, a flat, sandy strip of land. Jerusalem was built of stones, with not a single brick in it, but Babylon was built of brick, made out of common clay and molded by machinery. God made the rocks and man made the bricks. Stones grew, but bricks are manufactured. The stones in Jerusalem were cemented together with lime burnt out of the live rock, but the bricks of Babylon were cemented together with slime or common mud. Lime is a type of divine love that cements the living stones in the temple of God; but slime is a type of human policy, selfish motives, which bind together the oath-bound societies of wicked men. Jerusalem was made to be the home of the saints, the refuge of people that had the character of righteousness and peace; but Babylon was the home of apostates, the backslidden descendants of Noah, and has always been used as the type of apostasy and the home of backsliders. Jerusalem is to be rebuilt with precious stones, spoken of in several places in prophecy, and also the New Jerusalem is being built up in Heaven, the city of pure gold. On the other hand, Babylon is to go down in everlasting destruction and sink as a stone in the waters, to rise no more forever. There is harmony in all the ways of God.

The contrast between Nimrod and Melchizedek is no greater than the contrast between Babylon and Jerusalem. In the history of both of these cities we have the progress and the consummation and the everlasting destiny of apostates on the one hand, and true, persevering believers on the other hand.

21

The First Words on Justification by Faith

We have in the 15th chapter of Genesis the first words in the Bible on the subject of justification by faith, which makes this one of the great epochal portions of Scripture bearing on the revelation of the saving grace of God. Of course men had been justified by faith from the very beginning of human history, for Abel received the approval of God for his sacrifice, and Enoch had the testimony that he pleased God, and Noah had been pronounced a man that was perfect in his generation. All these and many others had believed in God, and had been justified and received the perfect assurance of their salvation. But what I mean is, that this 15th chapter is the first place in Scripture where the doctrine of justification by faith is distinctly made known and recorded for the enlightenment of all succeeding generations.

"The word of the Lord came unto Abram in a vision, saying, Fear not, Abram: I am thy shield, and thy exceeding great reward." These words about the shield and the reward must be taken in connection with what happened in the previous chapter. Abram had many foes, for the armies that he had slain up at Merom were his enemies, and then the king of Sodom was not his real friend, so that there were open enemies and subtle, secret enemies. Hence God assured Abram that He would be a divine shield around him to protect him from all sorts of foes, whether open or secret. We are told of an electric fish that can electrify the water around it in the ocean to such a degree that no other fish can enter the electrified zone, and by this method this fish protects itself from all its enemies. This illustrates how God can be like an electrified zone around His true children and protect them in an invisible way from their enemies.

The word "reward" must be understood in connection with the fact that Abram restored Lot and his family back to their home in

Sodom, and gave all the spoils to the king of Sodom, except the tenth, which he had given as an offering to Melchizedek. Thus Abram was left without any reward for himself to pay him for his services in capturing and restoring Lot and the other inhabitants of Sodom. Hence God promised that He would be Abram's reward in this matter, and that Abram could look to God alone for everything without depending on his fellow men.

Then follows the account of the promise of a son to Abram that should be his true heir, but the birth of that son, as well as all other favors, depended on the condition of Abram's faith. And the Lord brought Abram forth abroad and said, "Look now toward heaven, and tell the stars, if thou be able to number them: and he said unto him, So shall thy seed be." And Abram believed in the Lord, and the Lord counted it, that is, his faith, to him for righteousness. This is the great passage that the Apostle Paul uses so much in Romans in his argument on justification by faith. In this connection we need to grasp a clear perception of the two kinds of seed that God promised to Abram, the one referring to his fleshly posterity, and the other to his spiritual posterity. In chapter 13, when Abram was separated from Lot, God promised to make Abram's "seed like the dust of the earth." That promise was in special connection with giving Abram all the land that he could survey from Mt. Lebanon on the north to Beersheba on the south, and from the mountains of Moab on the east to the Mediterranean Sea on the west. And that promise had reference only to Abram's fleshly seed born of Abraham, Isaac, and Jacob.

Now in this chapter we have another great epoch in the life of Abram, another magnificent step in his pilgrimage of faith, which entered higher up into the spiritual life than ever before, and extended onward throughout all ages into the future destiny of Abraham's spiritual posterity. And hence in this passage we have "the star seed" promised to Abram, that "his children should be like the stars of heaven in multitude."

This promise of the star seed embraced only those who should have the faith of Abram, that is, should be justified by faith and be partakers of a heavenly and everlasting inheritance. No descendant of Abraham ever took part in the inheritance of the star seed except those that were justified by faith.

And also the promise embraces all the Gentiles who are justified by faith, and, as Paul argues in Romans, who become the spiritual children of Abraham by virtue of their faith in God. This shows the distinction between the fleshly children of Abram that are to inherit the land of Canaan, and be restored to that land in the coming age, and those other spiritual children who share Abraham's faith in Christ and are justified and partake of the heavenly inheritance, which embraces a place in the first resurrection, and in reigning with Christ over the whole world in the ages that are to come.

Just as the stars are superior to the dust on the earth, so the star seed of Abram are superior to the mere earthly seed, and have a much higher rank in God's plan concerning His kingdom in the ages that are to come. Jesus said that many should come from the east and west and north and south and sit down with Abraham, Isaac, and Jacob in the kingdom of Heaven. He refers to those believers among all nations and in all the various dispensations who had the faith of Abraham, Isaac, and Jacob, and that in the resurrection they, having the faith of those patriarchs, should share in their companionship and in their inheritance, showing how much the star seed are superior to the dust seed in their privileges.

Now notice how it is that the faith of Abram was accounted to him for righteousness. Abram did not have any real righteousness in himself and of himself, but when he, with all his heart, embraced the promise of Jehovah that he should have a son of his own, God accepted that faith in the place of righteousness, so that his faith was put down to his credit in the place of righteousness. It was his faith, Paul says, that was imputed to him for righteousness. This is the great secret of all justification, that men are to utterly ignore their own righteousness, and receive the Son of God, the Lord Jesus, as a personal Savior, and on the condition of their faith in Christ they are accepted as righteous, not because of their works, but because of their faith.

In the next place we must remember that this justification by faith took place before Abraham was circumcised, and while he was yet a Gentile, which proves, as St. Paul argues, that justification by faith took place before Abraham became a Jew, and while he was yet a Gentile. Hence justification by faith was not a Jewish doctrine, but a Gentile doctrine. It applies to all the Gentile nations that lie outside of the law of circumcision. Now you see as in the case of Melchizedek being the first priest among the Gentile nations before the Jewish priesthood was instituted, so the same is true of justification by faith, that it took place while Abraham was yet a Gentile, and thus has the priority over any special Jewish ceremony or covenant.

Now notice in the next place the witness to Abraham's faith, for he had said, "Whereby shall I know that I shall inherit it?" The Lord commanded him to offer a sacrifice, and to divide the pieces upon the altar, and to watch the sacrifice, that the fowls of the air should not devour it. As Abram sat there and drove away the fowls from eating the fresh meat on the altar, there came upon him a horror of darkness, which was prophetic of the terrible bondage that his children should go through for four hundred years in the land of Egypt. Abraham patiently endured the trying hour of that great darkness, and when he had complied with every condition that God required, then came the witness to his faith in the form of a smoking furnace and a burning lamp that passed between those pieces. The smoking furnace had special reference to the terrible sufferings of his posterity in bondage. And the burning lamp had special reference to their emancipation, the leaving of Egypt and the being constituted into an army that should march into Canaan as a living testimony to all nations of the covenant-keeping God Who had promised them that land. Here we have a prophetic incident which agrees exactly with the witness of the Holy Spirit to the true believer that receives Christ as his personal Savior.

If we analyze our experience of repentance and saving faith, and the sweet assurance of the Spirit to our justification, we find that all the points were set forth in the process of Abraham's justification, and the witness which sealed his faith and covenant. Faith is always tested and then honored. There is first the smoking furnace, and after that the burning lamp. This is God's method in dealing with His servants in all dispensations, both in His dealing with nations and with individuals. At the transfiguration there was a cloud, but out of that cloud there came a voice, "This is my beloved Son." It ought to inspire us with boundless confidence in every word of the Lord, that He arranges all things on one vast pattern, and if we stand true in the darkness, He will send the light. If we will patiently watch the cloud, out of it will come the voice. And if we, by the promises of God, will drive the vultures away from our sacrifice, by and by the sweet assurance will come.

There are millions in Paradise today who lived in this world, and prayed to God and were justified by faith, and received the sweet assurance of salvation. They never understood the doctrine about the subject, and never were enlightened concerning this 15th chapter of Genesis. But nevertheless the Holy Spirit led them through the process the same way He led Abraham. They received the results just the same as if they had been patriarchs or apostles.

This 15th chapter of Genesis and the writings of St. Paul are found to be in exact accord the one with the other. And the first words on the great subject of justification are as perfect as the last words, confirming the statement that Jesus Christ is the same yesterday, today, and forever.

22

Sarah and Hagar

Just as we have in the case of Abraham and Lot samples of the solar and the lunar saint, so we have in the case of Sarah and Hagar corresponding samples of the solar and the lunar church as brought out in the argument of St. Paul in Galatians. Paul argues that Sarah stands for the spiritual church, which is above and heavenly, and that Hagar stands for the legal church, which is earthly and human. But in the study of the 16th chapter of Genesis we find that these teachings are in their beginnings and not in their endings, which is brought out in later chapters. We see in this chapter a conflict between these two women, which has always been perpetuated between the church of the law and the church of the Spirit. But at the same time we see that the spiritual church did not reach its full emancipation at once, but had to struggle for a while with things that pertain to nature and to self.

The first lesson we have from this history is the effort that Sarah put forth to help God carry out His plan concerning giving Abraham a son. God had promised for many years that Abraham should have a son, a true heir, and that all the families of the earth should be blessed through that son. After waiting many years Sarah formed a plan to help God carry out His promise. But, as in all such cases, her planning brought trouble and disappointment. She thought within herself, "God has made a promise, but God has failed to fulfil His word, and now I must step in and help God out of His difficulty." And so you see in this chapter how she proposed to give her servant maid to be a wife to Abraham in order to secure the promised son. Sarah had not yet learned that great spiritual law, "that it is by faith and patience that we are to inherit the promises," as mentioned in Hebrews 6:12. Faith and patience are the two hemispheres in receiving the fulfillment of God's promises. Faith is instantaneous, but patience is gradual; faith is at first joyful, but patience has to endure much longsuffering; faith receives the promise, but patience is required to meet the conditions of the fulfillment. It is always indicative of a child mind to want a promise fulfilled immediately. When parents make a promise to a child, the child expects an immediate fulfillment of the promise. This was the case with Eve when God promised that her seed should bruise the serpent's head. She naturally supposed that her firstborn child was the promised Messiah, and when she saw her firstborn she said, "See, I have gotten the Jehovah man."

Every true believer must go through the process of learning to wait patiently on the Lord for the fulfillment of His word. And then how true it is that in the weakness of faith we attempt to help God to do His part of the work. Rachel followed the example of Sarah in this same matter of obtaining the promised children. Nature always rushes speedily to obtain its purpose, but true faith waits on the Lord for the appropriate moment for Him to work. When we attempt to do God's part of the work, He will stand still and let us work alone and fail; but when we resign the work to God and stand still, then the Lord takes the work in hand and brings it to pass. In a countless number of ways it comes out with us that we toil all night and catch nothing; but when the darkness is past and Jesus begins to work, then great and blessed results are speedily accomplished.

The first effect of Sarah's impatience about obtaining the promised child was that her maid became indignant at Sarah's authority and trampled upon the natural rights and authority of a mistress, so that Sarah became despised in her eyes. It always happens that when we lean on nature instead of the promises of God we come to grief and have to endure much humiliation.

The second effect of Sarah's impatience was to lose the sweetness of her spirit and lay the blame on her husband, though she herself had prompted him to the course of conduct which he had pursued.

The third effect of her impatience was to try to get rid of the evil in her own way, for it is said, "she dealt hardly with her servant maid," as if to force Hagar into a condition of humility and obedience. We never can deliver ourselves from the effects of our folly, and there is no way to remedy the evil consequences but to leave them in the hands of God and let Him manage us and take entire charge of both our folly and the effects of it.

The next lesson from this chapter is that St. Paul in his Epistle to the Galatians is inspired by the Holy Ghost to use these two women as types of two churches, the church of the law and the church of the Spirit. He tells us that Hagar represents the church in the earthly Jerusalem which was in bondage with her children, but that Sarah represents the church in the Holy Ghost, the heavenly city, which is the mother of all true spiritual believers.

23

The First Jew

We have another sample of some of the first words of God in Genesis 17, where we see how Abraham, who up to that time had been a Gentile, passed over into the zone of entire self-abandonment to God and became a Jew. The Apostle Paul gives us a definition of what a Jew is when he says, "He is a Jew who is one inwardly, and circumcision is that of the heart." Circumcision is never a type in the Bible of justification or the new birth, but always a type of the heart being separated from the flesh, and being filled with the power of Divine love. This is Paul's argument when he says that Abraham was justified by faith before he was circumcised. So that this chapter in Abraham's life supplies us with another epoch in his pilgrim journey from Ur of the Chaldees clear on through to the city which he saw in a vision, "which hath foundations, whose builder and maker is God." We have several remarkable words in this 17th chapter which will repay our study.

When Abraham was ninety-nine years old the Lord appeared unto him and said, "I am the Almighty God; walk before me, and be thou perfect. And I will make my covenant between me and thee, and will multiply thee exceedingly. And Abraham fell on his face: and God talked with him." This occurred five years after he received the clear, burning-lamp witness to justification by faith, and hence we have here steps in spiritual progress which are not to be confounded with the grace of pardon. Let me call your attention to some special points in this chapter.

1. Note the contrasts between chapters 15 and 17. In chapter 15 it says, "The word of the Lord came unto Abram," but in chapter 17 it says, "The Lord (Jehovah) appeared unto Abram." There is some difference between having the word of the Lord spoken to Abram in his inner being which he could understand, and then having a

Divine person and form which was none other than that of the Jehovah Angel, the Lord Jesus Christ in His pre-incarnate form, appear to Abram.

If this were the only case in Scripture of the kind, it might not be so significant. But if you will go through the entire Bible, you will find that God has made it a rule from the beginning of the world, to give His word and afterwards reveal His person. This is a wonderful thing in God's conduct with His people and well worthy of our notice.

We see that when Jacob was at Bethel he received the word of the Lord, spoken to him from Heaven, but twenty years later at Peniel he saw the Jehovah Angel face to face and called the place Peniel, which means the face of God.

And then when Moses was in the land of Egypt he certainly had the word of the Lord come to him. But forty years later, at the burning bush, he saw the living God of Abraham, Isaac, and Jacob in a clear manifestation.

The same was true in the life of Daniel, who heard the word of God many times in his earlier life, but later on saw the same form of the Lord Jesus standing on the bank of the river that John saw in the Isle of Patmos.

Jesus told His disciples that if they would believe in Him as perfectly as they did in God the Father, that He would reveal Himself to them and manifest Himself to them by the Holy Ghost. This is all a parable of what is now taking place, for in this Gospel age we believers must receive the Word of God as His true, inspired Word. And if we believe this Word, the day is coming when He shall appear again, and we shall see Him face to face and be transformed into His likeness, both body and soul.

2. In the 15th chapter Abram was commanded to slay certain animals and lay them on the altar as a sacrifice unto God. But in this 17th chapter he was commanded to use the sharp knife in cutting his own flesh. By this he offered himself as a living sacrifice to God, and passed into the zone of complete separation and the life of pure faith and love. By this Paul says he was sealed by the rite of

circumcision. In the first instance he offered animals in sacrifice, but in this instance he offered himself in sacrifice.

3. In chapter 15 Abram was a Gentile, and recognized the priesthood service of Melchizedek, who was God's great priest for all the nations of the world. But in this chapter Abram, for the first time in his life, becomes a Jew and receives in his own flesh the seal of the Jewish covenant. By the rite of circumcision he and his posterity were separated from all other nations on the earth, not only by a special covenant relating to his "dust" seed of earthly posterity, and of the "star" seed of his heavenly posterity, but also a separation in body from all other nations, which from that day to this is the mark of a real Jew according to the flesh.

This transaction by which Abram became a Jew was for the special purpose of separating one family from the earth in entire devotion to God distinct from all other nations. It was that they might set forth the truth of God to the world, and be a prepared people to receive the true Messiah, and, if they had been true to their covenant, to be God's missionaries and teachers to all of the other nations. It is by the baptism of the Holy Spirit and true circumcision of the heart that a Christian believer enters into the state of a true spiritual Jew.

4. Up to this time God had been known to Abraham as God and as Jehovah and the Most High God, a name which he learned from Melchizedek, but now in this chapter another name is given of God, and that is "El-Shaddai," which we translate "Almighty." This is the first time in the Bible that this name, "Almighty God," is used, and it is very significant. The Hebrew word "El-Shaddai" signifies the "All-sufficient God." The original word signifies an exhaustless fountain that pours itself out in everlasting fulness, without stint, without limit, without the possibility of being exhausted. The root word is used in various ways, as, for instance, sometimes it signifies a mother's breast, supplying an abundance of milk for the infant; and it also is used to signify a great spring gushing from the mountain side that never runs dry. The word could also be translated "the out-poured God," corresponding to the idea of Pentecost, the outpouring of the fulness of the Holy Ghost from the ascended Jesus, for Jesus is

the infinite Fountain, and out of Him is poured the everlasting river of the Holy Spirit.

Now please put this name, "El-Shaddai," the "All-sufficient God," "the outpoured God," in connection with the other words, "Walk before me, and be thou perfect." This shows that Abram had no strength in himself to accomplish such a thing or to enter into such a life, but that every step of that walk was to be attended by this Divine River, this out-poured Fountain, this everlasting presence of the "El-Shaddai."

It is beautiful to go through the Bible and notice the different names by which God reveals Himself. Every name that God uses of Himself reveals some new relation between God and man, or some new degree of manifestation of the Divine presence and character.

5. Let us notice the significance of the word which is translated "perfect," in "Walk before me and be thou perfect." The word "perfection" is never used in the Bible concerning the flesh, for the flesh is always in the Scriptures judged to death and banishment. But the word "perfect" is used in the Bible in connection with faith and hope and love, as where Paul speaks of perfect faith, and St. John speaks of perfect love. Love is not a thing of the flesh, but of the spirit, and love is shed abroad in the heart by the Holy Ghost. All the words in Scripture that we translate by the terms "perfect," and "holy," and "sanctify" are all derived from words in the original which signify separation, the putting of a thing in an unmixed condition, as gold without dross, and fire without smoke, and water without dirt. In the Greek translation of the Old Testament which was read by the Jews in the days of Christ, we find that this verse in the Greek Bible uses as the term for "perfect" a word which signifies "honey with the wax taken out of it." Our word "sincere" is a Latin word which means "honey without wax," and this is the word used in the Greek Bible for "perfect." Honey is a type of Divine love, and wax represents the fleshly mind. God commanded Abraham to walk under the power of "El-Shaddai," that is, in the power of the outpoured Spirit, and have no wax mixed up with the honey of his spiritual life in the heart.

So far as we can judge from his life, Abraham was a perfect believer before this 17th chapter, but we do not know the elements in his experience. But whatever may have been the depth or the degree of his inner spiritual life previous to this, here it would seem God settles the matter with Abraham. From now on his heart is to be entirely possessed with the honey of God's love, and his inner spiritual being is to be swayed by the Holy Spirit, liberated from the natural wax of his own nature.

6. We have the change of Abram's name to that of Abraham, which is only another feature in this great event in his life by which he enters the zone of a true, sublime, spiritual Jew. The name Abram signifies "a father," and the word "Abraham" is in the plural form and signifies "a multiplied father, a high father, a father of many nations." The changing of a name is always indicative of a great change in one's nature, and it is never accidental. We can learn many things by the instances in Scripture in which people's names were changed.

The word "Adam" is a Hebrew word and signifies "a man of the earth," and this is the first name used in Genesis 1:26. Later on in Genesis 2:23 the original word for man is "Ish," which signifies "the higher, the spiritual man, the man of a high personality." This name was not given to Adam until after the formation of Eve out of his rib, which is significant; for with the name Adam he was alone, but when his name became Ish he was not alone, but had his wife with him.

The word "woman" was used of Adam's wife, and the original word simply means "a female man." But later on when God promised that her seed should bruise the serpent's head, she was called by a new name, Eve. This signifies, "the mother of the living one," that is, the mother of the Messiah; so that the change of name had a wonderful significance.

The change of Jacob's name at Peniel has become familiar to all Bible students as a significant fact, marking an epoch in his religious life by which he entered the realm of prevailing prayer and became a prince of God. When Rachel was dying at the birth of Benjamin, she named her infant Benoni, the "son of my sorrow." But Jacob afterwards changed his name to Benjamin, which means "the son at my right hand." This was of prophetic significance, for Jesus on the cross was the Son of sorrow, and when He died in sorrow, in a certain sense the old Jewish mother died also. But when Christ rose and ascended to the right hand of God, He became in reality God's Benjamin, the Son at God's right hand.

Saul of Tarsus was named after the first king of Israel, but when he became an apostle in the power of the Holy Ghost his name was changed to Paul, showing the difference between his natural sectarian name as a Jew, and his apostolic name as a Christian and an apostle of the Lord Jesus. So that this changing of the name from Abram to Abraham was not a trifling matter, but one of those inspired words of God which characterize an epoch in the spiritual life of God's servant.

And also in this connection the wife of Abraham had her name changed from Sarai to Sarah. The word "Sarai" means "Jehovah is my Prince," but the word "Sarah" means "princess," showing that the princely character had now passed over from Jehovah to His servant and handmaid. The Hebrew words "Isra" and "Sarah" are the same words. Isra is masculine and means "a prince" and Sarah is feminine and means "a princess." When Jacob's name was changed to Isra-el, it means "a prince of God." The changing of Sarah's name corresponds exactly with the change of Jacob's name, only the suffix "El" is not attached to the name of Sarah as it was to the name of Israel. We will see the import of this changing of Sarah's name later on when we come into that part of Scripture where God chose to use her as a type of the true spiritual church.

Now if we put all these things together we will have a constellation of spiritual truths that gather around this event in which Abraham passed from a Gentile into a Jew, in which his spiritual life took higher ground, and he entered into a more definite and heavenly covenant with Jehovah. All this was needful to take place before the birth of Isaac, for it was in Isaac that his seed should be called. And it was with the birth of Isaac that there began to be that marvelous history which characterized the Jew as distinguished from all other nations in the world, and also distinguished from all other families that worshiped the true God.

24

The First Escaping from the Fire

In the destruction of Sodom we have a prophetic event concerning the final judgment of the world, and in the escaping of Lot and his daughters from the fire we have a prophetic sample of the catching away of the righteous before the letting loose of the great tribulation judgments upon the world. Hence chapter 19 in Genesis is a significant portion of Scripture bearing on the coming of the great tribulation and the rapture of the saints, and other things incidental to that period.

This world is to have two great world-wide baptisms, one of water and the other of fire, and these two baptisms are typical of the baptisms which God gives to His people. According as things are put down in the Bible, God deals with earth and man just alike. The world and man are identified together far beyond the ordinary conception of Christian people. The earth and man rise together or fall together; they were created together, they were cursed together, they were redeemed together, they will be judged together, and the everlasting destiny of earth and man is associated together throughout all coming ages.

Peter speaks of the two great baptisms of water and of fire. The first baptism by water destroyed all the sinners from the earth, and the second baptism by fire, we are told, will burn up the works, that is, the proud, carnal works of men. This agrees exactly with the Scriptures, that by the washing of regeneration our sins are taken from us, and then by the baptism of the Holy Ghost and fire our own works of the carnal self are destroyed, setting us free from our own works which are of the flesh.

Now we have in this 19th chapter of Genesis the first instance recorded in the world of the Lord's people making their escape from the judgment of fire and being protected from that awful curse.

Jesus tells us that His second coming will be like it was in the days of Sodom. Hence if we notice the various points in connection with the destruction of Sodom, we will have a prophetic picture of what is to come in relation to the return of our Lord and the judgment day.

1. Sodom was not destroyed until its cup of iniquity was full and the cry of it ascended to Heaven. This will be true at the winding up of the present age, when the rejection of Christ by the people of the world will reach its legitimate culmination. The principles of antichrist will so ripen in the human race as to meet the conditions that Sodom was in and the cup of human transgression will be full. And that will mark the hour for the coming of the Lord.

2. Just before the destruction of Sodom it was a time of peace and great prosperity. There was no war going on at the time, and the Scriptures refer to the fact that the people of Sodom were feasting and had a fulness of bread. They were living in luxury, pride, fleshly lusts, and everything was like a carnival of pleasure and prosperity. According to the words of Christ, such will be the condition of the world at His second coming. A great many people thought that Christ might come during the recent great European war, but they failed to notice the words of Scripture by Paul and Jesus, that when Christ comes the people of the world will all be saying "peace and safety." And then there are other Scriptures that show that the world will be in a condition of great commercial prosperity and the nations will be getting fat on wealth and pleasure and godlessness previous to their destruction. So this shows us the perfect agreement between the condition of Sodom just before its destruction and the condition this world will be in at the coming of the Lord.

3. There were three distinct classes of people in relation to the destruction of Sodom. There was Abraham, the man of perfect faith. He was living a life of separation, not only from the ungodly heathen, but also from the weak servant of God, Lot and his family. And he was in such relation to God as to be prepared for any emergency that God might send. He is a perfect picture of those true believers who are walking with God in the Holy Ghost, in a life of entire devotion and separation, and will be prepared to meet the Lord when the cry goes forth that the Bridegroom cometh.

Then there was a second class represented by Lot, who was a believer. The Scriptures pronounce him a righteous man, and he was delivered from the fire, but in what way? The word "righteous" and the word "justification" are both translated from the same word in the original Greek. From this we learn that Lot was a justified man, one who had his sins forgiven, but that is the strongest term that the Bible ever uses in connection with Lot. Everything goes to show that he did not enter into a state of complete consecration, and knew nothing of those deeper experiences of heart crucifixion and a life of perfect faith and communion with God.

You notice in the chapter that Jehovah Himself visited Abraham and talked with him, but the Lord sent two angels to deliver Lot. The Lord did not go to visit Lot, for it distinctly says that when He left Abraham He went up. Now see the difference between the personal Jehovah going to Abraham, but sending His angels to rescue Lot. And then notice that these angels had to seize hold upon Lot and drag him out of the city lest he should be burned. So that while he was saved, he was scarcely saved, and all his property and belongings were burned up. This sets forth exactly the condition in which great multitudes will be at the coming of the Lord; they will be delivered with great difficulty and be saved so as by fire, but will never take rank with those believers who are watching and ready for the Lord to come.

In the third class of people we see the people of Sodom and Lot's wife were either burned or turned to a pillar of salt. These set forth the character and condition of all the ungodly in the world who will not be even in a state of repentance, but will be found full of their iniquity when the Lord returns.

If this were the only place in Scripture where these three classes were set forth it might not signify so much, but when we find that this is only the first place in the Bible setting forth these three classes, and that there are many other places where the same facts are set forth, it is worthy of our consideration. In the army that Gideon had there were three classes, for we see there were twenty-two thousand that publicly confessed that they were cowards and would not fight and returned home. Then there were ten thousand that professed they had faith and courage and were willing to fight, but they did not measure up to the requirements for the front rank soldiers. Then we see in the three hundred a class of men that met the conditions, not only of heroism, but also of perfect diligence and faith and obedience. They were the ones chosen for the destruction of the Midianites, and are a sample of the front rank believers who will take part with Christ in the destruction of the armies of antichrist, as is prophesied in Isaiah 9:4, 5.

We find another case of the three kinds of people in the parables of Jesus concerning the pounds, for there we see the faithful ones in the first class, the ten-pounder and the five-pounder, who received large rewards. And then in the next class we see the unfaithful servant who hid his pound in a napkin and was condemned as an unbeliever. And then the king called for those rebellious sinners, the people in the third class, and they were condemned to be slain, as will be the case in the final battle of Armageddon.

And then we see the three classes set forth in the words of Jesus about the three kinds of branches, for some branches bore no fruit, and some bore some fruit, and other branches were purged and bore much fruit.

Another historic case is found in connection with Israel, for there we see that the Egyptians were drowned in the sea, and the weak, unbelieving Israelites died in the wilderness, but the true and faithful servants entered into Canaan and possessed the land.

Now if you think that all these cases in which the three different kinds of people are represented are an accident in the Bible, you are surely a long way from grasping the mind of God.

4. We see that Lot and his daughters must of necessity make their escape from Sodom before the angels turned loose the fire for its destruction. This agrees with all other Scriptures on the subject, that the righteous must make their escape from this earth before the coming of the great tribulation judgments on the world. There are some who teach that the true church of Christ will pass through the great tribulation. But I have searched every passage in the Bible bearing on that subject, and I find in every single case the righteous

will make their escape before the coming of the real judgment tribulation on the earth.

The rain did not begin to fall until after Noah and his family were shut in the ark, and the fire did not fall on Sodom until after Lot made his escape, and the Roman armies did not destroy Jerusalem until after the Christians had made their escape to some mountains on the east side of the Jordan. And Isaiah tells us that God will call for His people and hide them in their chambers until the destruction or desolation is past. So we may depend upon it that while it is true, as Jesus tells us, the true church may be on the earth during the beginning of sorrows, or as the Greek has it, "the preliminary birth pains," yet the real judgment day upon the nations will not begin until the true spiritual church has been caught away to meet the Lord Jesus in the air.

5. We must again notice the high rank of Abraham in connection with the destruction of Sodom in contrast with the weak and mixed condition of Lot. St. Peter tells us that "the righteous will be scarcely saved," but in the next epistle he speaks of the perfect believer, like Abraham, who "receives an abundant entrance into the everlasting kingdom of our Lord." If you will notice the words used in the first chapter of 2 Peter you will see that the believer described in those verses takes rank in everything with Abraham. It is said that he "has escaped the corruption that is in the world," and that "he has given all diligence to add to his faith virtue, and knowledge, and temperance, and patience, and godliness and brotherly love. And these things are not only in him, but they abound in him, and he has made his calling and election both sure. Hence there is for him an abundant entrance into the kingdom." Any one can see the contrast between such an apostolic believer and a feeble believer who is all mixed up with the world, and has barely enough grace to escape the fire of judgment.

And then again you notice that it was Abraham that prayed Lot out of the fire, for it is said that God remembered Abraham in connection with delivering Lot. This agrees with all Paul says, that ye which are strong must bear the infirmities of those who are weak. The full believer in Jesus must be ready to pray for and help the weaker members of the body of Christ and, like Abraham, fight their battles, and rescue them from the enemy, and bring them back from captivity, and serve them in various ways. The bridehood saints are those who have such union with the Lord as to be ministers of grace to weaker ones. They receive a full reward, as mentioned by St. John, in contrast with others whom Paul says will lose their reward and be saved, yet so as by fire (1 Cor. 3).

Here we see in this first instance of the people of the Lord being saved from judgment fire, a sample and an outline of all those things that will take place at the second coming of the Lord.

25

The First Words on the Second Birth

In the birth of Isaac we are given a perfect photograph of the new birth which we receive by faith in Christ. If any one does not have clear light on the new birth, and he will study closely the things mentioned in connection with the birth of Isaac, he can gather a perfect and infallible picture of the Bible doctrine of regeneration in such a degree that there need never be any confusion or misunderstanding on the subject. The book of Genesis is filled with samples and patterns of the way God does things from the beginning of the creation clear down to the end of time, both of things in the natural world and in the spiritual world in the old and the new creation. This record is given in Genesis 21. Let us put together the following points:

1. Isaac was the second child born in Abraham's family and, as I have said, a perfect type of the second birth which we receive by faith in Christ. Ishmael had been born about fourteen years previous to the birth of Isaac. Paul tells us he was born according to the flesh, according to the natural laws of generation. It required no faith, no special prayer, no special divine intervention for the birth of Ishmael, for the whole thing was of the flesh. His birth is exactly such a kind as we receive in our first birth from our parents, for it is entirely natural, without any of the miraculous in it or without any supernatural grace connected with it.

But in the birth of Isaac we have a sample of our second birth which must of necessity take place after our first natural birth. The Apostle Paul announces it as a fixed law in the ways of God, first that which is natural, and afterwards that which is spiritual. Hence we see there is a necessity for our receiving a second birth after our natural birth. This is emphasized in a wonderful way by the words of Jesus, that we must be born again, born from above, born the second time. Without this second birth it is impossible for us to see the Kingdom of God.

2. The birth of Isaac was brought about in a supernatural way, above and beyond the ordinary laws of nature or of human generation. We are told that Sarah was past age for bearing children, and hence God produced a miracle in giving life to the dead organs of Sarah's body by which she could become a mother. This is exactly what takes place in our second birth when we are regenerated by the Holy Ghost through faith in Christ. Our spiritual nature is dead in sin just as truly as Sarah's body was dead in old age. And just exactly as God touched the organs of her body into youth for the bearing of a son, so God by the Holy Ghost touches the dead organs of our spiritual nature by which a new life is produced in us, a life of divine love, a life of Christ which is above and beyond our natural Adamic life, a life that is as superior to our flesh as Christ is superior to sinful man.

The new birth can never be an evolution or a development from the natural man. Evolution or development can never change the nature of anything or the substance or the life of anything, for it can never be anything but the unfolding of that which is there originally. It is just as impossible for a sinner or a man in his natural condition to develop within himself a spiritual life, a new, divine life, as it is for an onion to evolve itself into an orange, or for a bird to develop itself into an angel. Hence we have in the supernatural power manifested by the birth of Isaac a sample of the exact kind of supernatural power put forth in the regeneration of a penitent sinner by faith in Christ.

3. The birth of Isaac was conditioned on Abraham's faith. We have seen in a previous chapter that when God promised Abraham a true son to be his heir it is said Abraham believed in the Lord, he accepted the words that God spoke to him, and on the condition of that faith in due time Isaac was born. This is exactly the case with us; it is by faith in Christ as a condition that we receive our second birth wrought in us by the Holy Spirit. Faith did not produce the life of Isaac, but faith was the condition, and it was God Himself that produced the child. It is not our faith that gives us the new birth, but our faith in Christ as a personal Savior is the condition

upon which the Holy Spirit works in us that sweet and marvelous change in our affections and desires which forms the greatest epoch in our lives in this world.

It has been marked a long time ago that faith receives and love gives. Faith takes in the promise and then love is born and pours itself out. Faith takes in Christ and love pours itself out in serving Him. Isaac was born through faith, and then afterwards he poured himself out in service and laid down his own life on the altar. Thus we see in every way we turn the picture around, that all the facts connected with the birth of Isaac are reproduced in the second birth which the believer receives by believing on the Lord Jesus.

4. From the hour that Isaac was born he became the true heir of Abraham and had the dominion and the authority in the home over Ishmael, who was the firstborn. This is exactly true of our second birth, that from the time we are regenerated by the Holy Spirit our new birth becomes the true heir. The life of Christ which comes into us by the second birth has the dominion over our first birth, and over the things connected with our first birth. It is by the new man which is born in us that we become the heirs of God and joint heirs with Christ to a heavenly inheritance. If Isaac had never been born Ishmael would have inherited everything that Abraham possessed; and so if we are not born the second time we simply inherit the possessions of our father Adam. But when Isaac was born there was a change in the inheritance, and from that time on Isaac became the true heir to inherit everything that Abraham had. Now in like manner when we are born the second time, it is our new life that becomes the true heir, and we are joined on to Christ to share His inheritance in all the possessions, both in Heaven and in earth.

There is nothing in all the world that can take the place of being born, for it is out of our birth that we possess our personality and our gifts and our capabilities and our destiny. And of all the things connected with being born nothing is so high or great or has in it such capabilities and destiny as being born of God. It is the great miracle of grace. It is the starting point on the new creation. It is the seed corn out of which will come at last the new heavens and the new earth.

26

The First Words on Purging Out the Old Leaven

We have in the 21st chapter of Genesis the first place in the Bible where the Scripture doctrine is set forth on purging out the old fleshly leaven. The great Dr. Chalmers preached a celebrated sermon on "the expulsive power of a new affection" which for many years has been a classic in pulpit literature. The incident recorded in this chapter, on expelling the fleshly child Ishmael out of the family of Abraham, is a remarkable illustration of the expulsive power of a new affection, or of what the Apostle Paul terms in his Epistle to the Corinthians, "the purging out of the old leaven that ye may be a new lump." The incident occurred when Isaac was about two or three years old, at the time that he was weaned. It formed another epoch in the life of Abraham almost as significant as the birth of Isaac.

At the birth of Isaac there was the incoming of a new life in the home, a life characterized by supernatural marks, and a life of spiritual force as a special gift from God. At the time that Isaac was weaned there was the outgoing of an old life, a life that was fleshly in all its import and power, without any elements in it of spirituality. The incoming of the new life was a birth, but the outgoing life was a death in its significance. When the new life comes in it is a sum in addition, but when the old life goes out it is a sum in subtraction, and both of these parts of arithmetic were wonderfully manifested in the records of this 21st chapter of Genesis. In order to understand more clearly the purpose of this incident, let us notice the following points:

1. We read that Ishmael, who was at this time about fifteen years old, mocked the young child Isaac, by which we understand that he teased the child. Perhaps he destroyed his playthings, or made ugly faces at him, and in various ways manifested his envy and jealousy against Isaac, because he was the true heir of Abraham and the child

of Sarah. This mocking of Ishmael was very significant from a spiritual standpoint because it is referred to in the New Testament, and must be looked upon as one of the manifestations of the natural fleshly mind against a true spiritual life.

You will notice it is not said that Isaac persecuted Ishmael, but Ishmael persecuted Isaac, for it is always true that the flesh attacks and persecutes the things of the Spirit. There is not a single passage in the Bible where the spiritual mind attacks and opposes the flesh, but it is always the flesh taking the initiative and antagonizing the Spirit.

When the Israelites were marching towards Canaan they were attacked by the Amalekites, who were their cousins in the flesh, and the Amalekites opposed the progress of Israel in their journey to Canaan. In the case of Joseph and his brethren it was not Joseph that persecuted his brethren, but his brethren, through envy and jealousy, persecuted him. It was not Daniel that preferred charges against the princes, but the princes, in their envy and jealousy, preferred charges against Daniel. It was not Jesus that made the attack upon the Scribes and Pharisees, but they attacked Jesus and sought to slay Him.

This truth runs through the entire Bible and into all the experiences of Christian life. Whether it be in a family or a nation, or a visible church or human experience, always and forever it is the evil, fleshly mind that attacks the good mind and seeks to destroy the true spiritual life of Jesus. It was not God that ran away from Adam, but Adam ran away from God. There is something in the character of sin that makes it forever the antagonist of God and righteousness.

2. When Sarah observed Ishmael mocking and persecuting her little son Isaac, it aroused all the godly and just indignation of her upright and motherly heart to interfere and stop the offender from trespassing upon the rights and the life and the happiness of her child. This was all under the guidance of the Holy Spirit, and God made it the occasion for Sarah's taking the initiative in expelling the offender.

When Abraham returned home at the close of the day, Sarah said to him that he must "cast out the bond woman and her son, for the son of the bond woman should not be heir with her son Isaac." Those were the first words ever recorded in the Bible preaching the divine truth of expelling the carnal life and purging out the old leaven. Of course the saints of God in previous generations had been delivered in various ways from the fleshly nature, whether regarded in a domestic light or as a religious experience. But it so turns out that the words of Sarah to Abraham on expelling the fleshly child are the first words and the first time in all history where the doctrine as taught by Paul was announced as the will and plan of God.

You must remember it is in this connection that the Apostle Paul, in Galatians, teaches us that Sarah at that time became the representative of the true spiritual church of God, which contends for a life of entire devotion and the principle of holiness. She spoke those words to Abraham under the inspiration of the Holy Ghost, and as a prophecy in her rank as a type of the spiritual church, as Paul says, the Jerusalem which is above, which is the mother of us all.

I do not suppose that Sarah, in preaching that little sermon to Abraham, had any conception of the magnitude of her ministry, and of the immortal effects that her words would have on all subsequent generations. Little did she dream that the great Apostle Paul would incorporate her words into the New Testament, and make them standard words in the teaching of the Christian church. And because of her words she was chosen as a representative of the glorified church of the Lord Jesus Christ throughout all ages, and extending even into the New Jerusalem. When any one speaks under the guidance of the Holy Ghost he never knows the significance of his words or the vastness of their meaning.

It would seem that Abraham objected at first to the casting out of Ishmael, and thus purging the leaven of the flesh out of his home. But God spoke to Abraham and sanctioned the teaching of his wife and said, "Hearken to the voice of your wife in this matter of casting out the bond woman and her son." There is one case where God told the husband to obey his wife, and these words were spoken two thousand years before the Apostle Paul told wives to obey their husbands. I make no comments, I simply state facts, not to flatter Sarah or in the least to change the words of the apostle, but because Sarah was voicing the great doctrine of the true spiritual church of Christ.

3. It is enough to thrill the understanding with great admiration to see how God has arranged the teachings of Scripture in long lines of light from one end of the Bible to the other. The word "leaven" is always used in Scripture to represent the fleshly mind, the carnal reason, and it is never in a single place used to signify righteousness or love or holiness. The apostle taught the Corinthian church that one rotten apple would spoil the other apples in the same box. He demanded that that church should purge out a corrupt member because he would corrupt the church, and says, "Purge out the old leaven, that ye may be a new lump." In several places the same thing is taught, that the leaven of the fleshly mind must be put away, for it can never be improved or brought into the true service of God.

Now if you will look at that subject in the light of the Old Testament you will be surprised to notice the perfect oneness of God's Word running through both the Old and New Testaments. If you will travel through the great fruit orchards in California your eye will be thrilled with the beautiful sight of seeing in many places great long, straight rows of fruit trees, oranges or olives or other fruits. They stretch away a mile or more in length, and in such perfect uniformity of size as to form lines of living poetry, whether they are decked in vernal bloom or autumnal fruit. A similar effect is produced by looking into Scripture and seeing the great long lines of divine truth arranged in perfect order from the beginning to the end of the Bible.

Now you take this sermon that Sarah preached to Abraham on expelling the old leaven of a fleshly life, and see how it is set forth in other Scriptures. We read, "Thou shalt not sow thy vineyard with divers seeds: lest the fruit of thy seed and the fruit of thy vineyard be defiled" (Deut. 22:9). If different seeds are sown in the garden in close proximity which have contrary elements in them, as, for instance, the gourd and the tomato, the bloom of the plants will fertilize and pollute the true nature of the plant and the fruit. Hence God taught the Hebrews that in their garden they must learn the lesson of separation, and not have contrary fruits in close proximity to avoid any pollution of one with the other.

In the next verse it is said: "Thou shalt not plow with an ox and an ass together." The ox is a clean animal and works with a yoke on his neck, but the ass is an unclean animal and works with a collar on his neck. You see, the two animals are contrary to each other in their nature and in their walk and in their mode of pulling the plow. This was not written on account of the animals especially, but on account of the Israelites, that if they wanted to serve God they must not hitch up the old Adam and the Lord Jesus to the same plow to carry on their religious farming. When contrary elements are mixed it always works damage and especially damage to the good side, whether in the heart or in the life or in business or in church enterprises.

In the next verse it is said: "Thou shalt not wear a garment of divers sorts, as of woolen and linen together." Wool is the product of an animal, and linen is the product of a vegetable, and you see that they possess contrary natures. If you wash a piece of wool for years and years you can never get all the grease out of it, and that is a type of the flesh, which can never be delivered from its true essential nature. Linen is entirely free from grease and is always used in Scripture as a type of the working of the Spirit, as a type of grace separated from sin.

Many centuries later the prophet Ezekiel told the priests that when they went to minister in the holy places they must not wear garments made of wool, which would cause them to sweat, but they must be dressed in pure linen. Sweat is a sign of the fall and sin, of bondage and slave labor. If Adam had never sinned there would never have been any sweat from a human body, because God mentioned the word "sweat" as a curse on Adam and a token of evil.

God wants us to worship Him in the spirit which agrees with the garments of pure linen, and in the freedom of the spirit of love and faith and hope, without the admixture of legality or bondage or religious slavery. The unmixed garment is to set forth the pure and unmixed worship of the heart. At the close of Revelation we are told that the bride of Christ was dressed in pure linen, clean and dazzling. There is no mention made of wool, but every word indicates the spiritual nature separated from the flesh.

Now just put all these things in the Bible in a straight row and see what a magnificent picture it sets forth of serving God and worshipping Him in a state of separation, and not having the service or the heart mixed up with contrary elements; and we will see that this first sermon that Sarah preached on separating the spiritual child from the fleshly child extends throughout all Scripture without any change or modification in the Word of the Lord.

How significant are the words that right in connection with the expulsion of the carnal child it is mentioned that Isaac was weaned, and that his father made him a great feast. Every one of these thoughts are perpetuated through the Bible. In Psalm 131 it is set forth that the weaning of a child from its mother's milk is a picture by which God teaches that the believer is to give himself up in entire devotion to the Lord. He is to have his heart weaned from the things of this world so that it does not crave the things of earth or of the old self, but is so weaned from them as to be satisfied with the things of God and with His will and His plan in our lives. The same truth is referred to by the apostle in Hebrews 5:12-14 where he shows the difference between a baby Christian who feeds on milk and a strong, purified believer that is able to eat solid food. The words "strong meat" are literally "solid food," that is, food that must be chewed in contrast with liquid food which a baby drinks. Thus you see that the weaning of Isaac at the time of expelling the old leaven was an incident teaching the believer advancing from a state of religious infancy into the zone of a victorious believer.

And then notice also the fact that Abraham made a great feast for Isaac at the same time. Isaiah prophesied that the Lord would make a great feast for His people. This doubtless referred to the outpouring of the Holy Spirit upon the infant church and giving those believers a great feast of joy and gladness, although the prophecy of Isaiah may have a still later fulfillment in the final restoration of Israel in the kingdom period.

We see in conclusion that the first words that Sarah preached to Abraham on purging out the old leaven hold steady throughout all Scriptures. The final statement of apostolic teaching on that subject is of the same nature and scope as those first words uttered by Sarah in the beginning of religious doctrine.

27

The First Offering Up of the Beloved Son

We have in Genesis 22 for the first time in the Bible a great picture of God offering up His beloved Son as a sacrifice for the sins of the world. This account of Abraham offering up Isaac did not take place for the sake of Isaac or for the sake of Abraham, but on account of the Lord Jesus Christ, the beloved Son of the Father. Take away the offering up of the Son of God and the whole history sinks into insignificance, and perhaps incredulity. It is Christ that gives life and truth and significance to all these histories that were arranged in a specially prophetic manner, setting forth the things concerning Christ.

Where we read that God did tempt Abraham, it should read, "God did test Abraham," that is, put him to a trial for the perfecting of Abraham's faith and character, but more particularly as a pattern of what God Himself would do in offering up His only begotten Son. The test of a man's faith and obedience is always in ratio to the man's character and person and capacity. That which would be a great trial to one person might be a small trial to another. And so God, in dealing with His servants, works on a large scale. He distributes the testings and trials with infinite wisdom according to the magnitude of the soul He is dealing with, and according to the vocation that the believer follows in life, and in relation to the church and the Kingdom of Heaven.

History does not record any greater test of a man's faith and obedience in the whole world than that which was required of Abraham. And if we are to measure the magnitude of Abraham's person and character and the place he follows in the plan of God by the dealings that God had with him, we do not find a greater character in human history than that of Abraham in connection with the office and work that he followed. Let us notice some of the details in this great picture of offering up the beloved son.

1. We see that Abraham took Isaac and some servants along with him and traveled three days, until they came in sight of Mt. Moriah, which is the place of Jerusalem. Then Abraham left his servants with the asses to wait for him while he and Isaac went on up the mountain to the place of sacrifice. This shows that although the servants were servants of God, and doubtless in a state of saving grace, as they had been trained in Abraham's family, yet they were not suitable to go up the mountain to see the slaying of Isaac. Perhaps they had not the strength or faith to endure the sight, and had they gone it is likely their faith would have broken down and they would have rebelled, and that would have spoiled God's plan. Those servants went as far as it was needful for them to go, and as far as their spiritual capacity would endure. But Abraham and Isaac were of a higher order of faith and could follow God into regions of abandonment and sacrifice away beyond the dreams of those servants, although they were religious men.

Now this is a truth brought out in subsequent portions of Scripture, especially in the crucifixion of Christ. Jesus told His own disciples that they would all forsake Him at the time He was crucified, and the words of Christ were fulfilled. Now the disciples were true believers, and in a state of grace, and on their way to the heavenly kingdom. We have many proofs that they had been pardoned, and Jesus affirms several times that they were the children of God, their heavenly Father. Yet none of those disciples had reached a state of experience which enabled them to follow Christ all the way to the cross. They could go a certain distance, up to the measure of their spiritual strength, and beyond that they broke down and forsook the blessed Jesus before reaching the cross. So that when we see Abraham leaving his servants at the foot of the mountain it corresponds exactly with the disciples following Jesus a certain distance and then forsaking Him.

2. Abraham bound the wood and put it on Isaac's shoulder for him to carry up the mountain to the place of sacrifice. This agrees exactly with the fact that Jesus bore His own cross. Isaac carried the

very wood upon which he was to die and be burned, and so Jesus carried the very cross on which He was crucified. In how many ways this fact sets forth the truth that each believer is commanded by the Lord Jesus to take up his own cross and follow Christ.

The cross may have a different form and consist of a different thing for each believer, and what is a real cross to one might not be a cross to another. But whether it is something material or spiritual, or something in the believer or something in his circumstances, it is always something on which the believer is to die and yield up his ambitions and plans and self-will. There is to be a death, a real inward death, upon that thing which constitutes our cross. That which was true of Isaac and of the blessed Son of God must be true of all genuine whole-hearted followers of Christ in this life of faith.

3. We notice that Abraham carried the fire and the knife in his own hand, for there was a sufficient reason for not letting Isaac carry the fire and the knife. This truth was carried out in the crucifixion of Jesus, for it was God the Father that held in His own power the fire and the knife in relation to the crucifixion of Jesus. The fire is a real setting forth of God's wrath and judgment against sin. Jesus took the place of the lost sinner, and, furthermore, He not only took the sinner's place, but according to the original words in the Hebrew and Greek, He took the place of sin itself. God dealt with His dear Son on the cross as if He had been a bundle of sin. The apostle said He was made sin for us. Mark you, He was not made a sinner, for while He was made in the likeness of sinful flesh, He was not made a sinner. But He was made sin, that is, He took the place of sin, and He endured the burning wrath of God against sin, which corresponded exactly with the fire that Abraham carried, expecting to burn up his own son. The sharp knife that Abraham bore was a setting forth of the law of God, for the law is compared to a two-edged sword, or a sharp knife, and it was the sharp edge of God's law that pierced the blessed Jesus and caused His death. Thus we see that Abraham performed the offices toward Isaac that God the Father performed toward His dear Son in His sacrifice on the cross.

4. There is much significance in the way that Abraham answered the inquiry of Isaac when he said, "Father, here is the fire and the

knife and the wood, but where is the sacrifice?" If you peep under-neath the veil that covers Abraham's answer you will see that in his reply there is revealed the true way of setting forth the love of God as the great power that draws us into the crucifixion of self. If Abraham had replied to Isaac in a severe and rugged manner that he intended to slay Isaac as a sacrifice it doubtless would have been a premature shock to the young man and led to serious results. But Abraham replied to Isaac in such a tender and gentle way, drawing his mind away from self to God, and showing that God was a being of infinite love and providence, and that at the right time God would provide the appropriate sacrifice.

I think we can read between the lines and hear Abraham preaching to Isaac as they ascended the mountain a marvelous sermon on devotion to God, on loving God, on wanting to please Him to such an extent that we should be willing to lay down our lives for the Lord. By the time they reached the place of sacrifice Isaac was per-fectly willing to be bound and consented to be slain to fulfil the pur-pose of God. Something like this must have been the case, because there is no hint that Isaac rebelled against his father or refused to be bound, although he was a lad of about fifteen years of age, and certainly old enough to resist the father if he had not been filled with the same faith and love that the father had.

Now this throws a stream of light on the offering up of the blessed Jesus, because it was in a sea of tender, pure, boundless love in which Christ offered up Himself to die. Jesus did not have His eye on the rugged cross or on the nails, but more especially He had His eyes on poor lost sinners and on their need of a Saviour, and on the infinite love that the Father had for a lost world, and on the infinite joy that would come to Him as a result of dying for sinners. And so it was the love side that Jesus saw in being offered up upon the cross. Have we lived long enough to see these things, or to learn them, or to have them take possession of our hearts? Have we learned to approach the altar of self-sacrifice, not from "the raw head and bloody bones" standpoint, but from the side of tender compas-sion and love, with our eyes on the love of God and the love of Jesus and love for souls and love for Christ's coming and His Kingdom and His glory that shall fill the earth?

It was love that led Abraham to preach such a tender sermon to Isaac as not to frighten the child, but to win him to a willingness to die. It was love that God the Father preached to His dear Son which led Jesus to offer Himself up in a sea of compassion and loving-kindness towards sinners. It is nothing but pure charity possessing our hearts that will make us willing to give up self, to expel the old leaven, to cast out the carnal thing, and to suffer not only without murmuring, but with a peculiar, strange, heavenly joy because we, like Jesus, can look through the darkness to the joy that is set before us, the joy of being like Christ, the joy of seeing Him as He is. All these things were magnificently set forth in Abraham's offering up his beloved son. And all these things were set forth in an infinite degree in God the Father offering up His dear Son to be the Saviour of sinners. And in our measure and up to our spiritual capacity these things will be repeated in our hearts and lives if we follow Jesus clear through to the end.

28

The First Words on the Resurrection

For the first time in the Bible we have the doctrine of the resurrection set forth in the words of Abraham to his servants, when he said to them that they should stay by the asses and wait while he and Isaac went up to the mountain top and worshipped, and then they would return again. Have you ever thought how in the world could Abraham use such words when he was intending to slay Isaac and then burn his body to ashes? In view of that fact how could he say that he and Isaac would worship and return to the servants and go back to their home at Beersheba? It would be impossible to understand that incident unless we had the added words of the apostle in the 11th chapter of Hebrews, that Abraham believed that after he had slain Isaac and burned his body, that God would raise him from the dead, so that he could truly fulfil his promise to the servants that they would return to them again.

You see the word "resurrection" is not used in the book of Genesis, but there are other words which imply the resurrection, and there are actions which signify and prophesy the resurrection, and these are equal to the use of the word "resurrection." Now we are sure that the doctrine of the resurrection was known to Adam and the early patriarchs clear down to the days of Abraham. They all believed that the dead would be raised. But what I mean is that Abraham's offering up of Isaac is the first place in the Bible where the resurrection is definitely referred to as an object of faith. You see Abraham believed a great deal more than the record in Genesis tells us about, for the apostle affirms positively that Abraham believed that God would raise Isaac from the dead after he had been slain and his body burned to ashes. And we know that the apostle spoke by the Holy Ghost. So we have a point in Abraham's faith revealed in the New Testament which is not mentioned in the Old Testament.

In the next place Abraham not only believed that the dead would rise again, but he believed in the first resurrection of the righteous as against the resurrection of all men in general. We know this from the fact that the apostle uses a little word in Hebrews which has often been overlooked by commentators and Bible students. There are two small words that are used in the Greek Testament in reference to the resurrection, but they are very significant.

Whenever the New Testament mentions the resurrection of the dead in a general way, the Greek speaks of the resurrection "of the dead," using the little word "ton," which we translate "of." This little word, the resurrection of "ton," of the dead, refers to the resurrection of all men. On the other hand, in every single passage where the resurrection of Christ and of the righteous are referred to the little Greek word "ek" is always used, that is, the resurrection "out from the dead" in contrast with the resurrection of the dead. The "ek" resurrection "from the dead" always indicates that certain persons will be resurrected and leave other persons still dead, whose bodies remain in the earth. Hence we always read of Jesus being raised "from the dead" and the righteous being raised "from the dead," and the first resurrection is "from the dead." Paul wanted to be conformed to Christ, that he might attain to "the out-resurrection, which is out from among the dead," and not the resurrection of the dead as it is put in our common English Bible in the third chapter of Philippians.

Now when the apostle says in Hebrews 11 that Abraham believed God would raise Isaac he uses that word "ek," "out from the dead," proving that Abraham believed in the resurrection out from the dead, that is, the resurrection of the righteous, which would take place before the resurrection of the ungodly. This shows us the vast amount of truth that God had revealed to Abraham's mind, a whole world of truth with regard to the sacrifice of the Son of God, and the first resurrection out from among the dead, as well as the reign of Christ on the earth, and the New Jerusalem, the final home of the glorified saints.

What a pity it is that so many commentators and Bible students have failed to notice the difference between the "ek" resurrection, "out from the dead," and the "ton" resurrection "of the dead." If those words had been noticed by all past Bible scholars and properly understood, it would have given the church so much more light on the pre-millenial coming of Jesus, and on the difference between the first resurrection of the saints, and the last resurrection of the wicked.

Another truth expressed by Abraham in his words to his servants should not be overlooked, and that is that the righteous dead, after being resurrected, are to come back with Jesus and live on this earth. He said to his servants that "I and the lad will go yonder and worship, and return." He expected to kill Isaac and burn his body and see him resurrected from the dead, and then they would both return to where the servants were, and go back to their home. This certainly shows that Abraham had faith in the teaching that the saints of God, after being resurrected, are to return back to this world. That shows that the faith of Abraham in that direction extended away beyond the ordinary faith of professing Christians.

There is another very significant passage in regard to the Kingdom of Heaven which is to come upon this earth after the resurrection of the saints. After God had proved Abraham's obedience and told him not to touch his son, but to offer up the ram in the stead of his son, then the Angel Jehovah said to Abraham, "Because thou hast done this thing, and hast not withheld thy son, thine only son, that in blessing I will bless thee, and in multiplying I will multiply thy seed as the stars of the heavens, and as the sand which is upon the seashore."

I have spoken in previous chapters of the great significance of Abraham's "dust" seed and "star" seed, and called attention to the fact that the "dust" seed was promised first in relation to Abraham's fleshly posterity owning Palestine, and then the significance of the "star" seed, which is his spiritual posterity, in possessing the heavenly kingdom. Now notice we are now studying that the "star" seed are mentioned first and the "dust" seed are mentioned second, which is exactly the way it should be. You see when the righteous are raised in the first resurrection and caught up to meet the Lord in the air, they will remain with Christ up in the sky until after the marriage supper of the Lamb, and then return with Jesus in open manifested glory to chain the Devil, destroy the anti-Christ, and reign on the earth. It is at that time, when Jesus returns in open manifested glory with His saints, that the Jews on the earth will see Him, and recognize Him Whom they have pierced. At that time all the Jews living on the earth will receive Him as their Messiah and Saviour. Then those saints who come back with Christ will be the "star" seed and they will take the priority. But those Jews living on the earth will be the "dust" seed and they come second. In the beginning the "dust" seed came first and the "star" seed came second, but at the end, when the Kingdom of Heaven shall come, then the "star" seed, the glorified saints, will come first and the "dust" seed, the Jews living on the earth, will come second.

Can you see the beat of it, how the words of the Bible are so placed with such exactness as to be infallible, not only in their truthfulness, but also infallible in the order, the time and the place in which the words occur and in which they will be fulfilled. In the time that is past it has been the Jew first, putting the Gentile last. But in the future dispensation the glorified believers in the church will come first and the Jew that is living on the earth will come next. Hence this is the way the words are placed in this 22nd chapter of Genesis.

29

Seeking a Wife for Isaac

We have in the 24th chapter of Genesis one of the most perfect prophetic types in the entire Old Testament of the way in which God the Father sends forth the Holy Spirit to search out from the saved ones a special company to compose the Bride of the Lamb. It is a long chapter, and the details that are recorded therein would never have been put in the Bible merely as a piece of history or as a biography of Rebekah as the wife of Isaac. Such a lengthy, detailed account would be out of all proportion to other subjects which are mentioned in Scripture. But when we study the chapter as a revelation of the Lord Jesus Christ and of His Bride, and the things connected with His coming and His Kingdom, then there is sufficient warrant for the lengthy account and all the little particulars that are given. Everything is great in proportion as it relates to Christ and constitutes a revelation of Him and His Kingdom. That is God's first word in relation to searching out a chosen company to form the Bride of the Lamb.

It is true in our lesson about Eve being the first bride we had occasion to bring out some points in which Eve was a prophetic picture of Christ's wife, but that lesson occurred before the Fall and does not fit in the same way that this lesson does in the 24th chapter. This is a lesson in grace and not in primitive holiness in Eden, and we will find a great many interesting things in this lesson which occur for the first time in the Bible. The things we will find as typifying Christ and His Bride go straight on through all the remaining part of the Bible without any change clear down to the last day, when there will be the glorious fulfillment of these first words. Will you please put together the following points and see how perfectly they set forth the things of Christ and the company of His true, elect saints?

1. It was after Isaac had been offered up as a sacrifice on Mt. Moriah that Abraham sent his servant to find a wife for him. This agrees with the fact that Christ was first crucified and rose from the dead and ascended to the right hand of God the Father, and then the Spirit was sent forth among all the nations of the earth to search out a company to constitute the Bride of the Lamb. In the Old Testament Jehovah is spoken of many times as a husband and the people of Israel are spoken of as His wife. But all such Scriptures are in connection with the kingdom of Israel on the earth, and in relation to Israel being chosen out from all other nations. Israel was never the wife of Jehovah in the heavenly sense, but always in an earthly sense. When the Jews crucified Christ they became thereby divorced from Jehovah as His wife. Then when Christ arose He began to search out a heavenly company for a heavenly Kingdom, and the Bride of Christ is to be a special company gathered out in the church age. This is taught by St. Paul where he says he espoused Gentile converts to the Lord Jesus.

2. In the person of Eliezer, the steward that had charge of Abraham's goods, we see a most beautiful type of the Holy Spirit as the Steward of the household of God, having charge of all the possessions that belong to Jesus, the heavenly Isaac. The word "Eliezer" means "God's helper," and so the name and the service that he performed agree exactly. We read that Eliezer had charge of all of Abraham's property and managed all his estate, and this is what the Scriptures teach concerning the Holy Spirit. He has been sent to administer on the estate of Christ, to be the Sanctifier and Comforter of believers, to apply the atoning blood of Christ to the heart, to reveal the Scriptures to the understanding, to teach and guide the believer into all spiritual truth, and to have charge of God's providence in the life of the believer.

3. Abraham gave orders to his steward not to take a wife for Isaac from the Canaan nations, but to go back to his own kindred and get a wife from his own blood relations. This agrees with all Scripture bearing on the subject, that the Bride of Christ is not gathered as raw material from the heathen nations or from sinners. But out of those people who become converted and are thereby in the great

household of God there is to be gathered a company of those who are willing and obedient to enter into a covenant of perfect consecration, and be sealed in perfect union with Jesus by the Holy Spirit on the condition of their appropriate faith.

It is after penitents are converted that the Holy Spirit makes overtures to them concerning a perfect consecration, and the entering into a covenant of entire devotion to God, and receiving Christ as a perfect Saviour that they may enter into the fellowship of the Holy Spirit. Thereby they become candidates for the bridehood company, or, as Paul puts it, become espoused to the Lord Jesus to be His wife at His second coming. Jesus teaches this when He shows the difference between the disciples of John, who were just beginning the life of faith, and His own disciples, whom He designates as "children of the bridechamber." We must first be born again and be members of God's kindred in order that we may be candidates to receive the baptism of the Spirit.

4. We notice that when Eliezer reached the well of water (verses 17-20) and requested of Rebekah a drink of water, that she at once obeyed his request, and not only gave him to drink, but also drew water for the camels. In performing that service she had no apprehension of the magnitude of her little ministry, but was simply acting out the courtesy and kindness of her nature and of her training. None the less that act of service formed the basis of Eliezer's choice and faith that she would be the one for the wife of Isaac. This same principle is carried out in the early service of a young convert. When we submit to the Lord Jesus Christ and trust in Him, we have no conception of the magnitude of that act. Little do we dream that our early service to the Lord will form the basis for great and wonderful things if we continue to follow Him.

It is very significant how many people in the Bible met their wives at a well of water. Eliezer met the wife of Isaac at the well of water, and then Jacob met Rachel at a well of water, and when Moses left Egypt he met Zipporah, his wife, at a well of water. Then Jesus, on His way through Samaria, met the woman of Samaria at a well of water. She was a marvelous type of the Gentile church receiving the Holy Spirit and being a missionary church, out of whom there is selected the Bride of the Lamb. These things were not an accident, and they are all put down in the Bible because they all belong to one great truth.

5. In response to Rebekah's service in drawing the water, Eliezer gave her a ring and a bracelet out of Abraham's treasures as a token of approval for her service. This corresponds with the fact that the believer receives at his justification a token from the Father by the Holy Ghost in the assurance of forgiveness and peace with God. The prodigal son on returning to the father received a ring, the token of reconciliation, and so this ring and bracelet given to Rebekah agrees exactly with the witness of the Spirit which we receive when we trust Jesus as a personal Saviour.

6. Eliezer on reaching Rebekah's home refused to enter the house until after he had told his mission and received a favorable response, as we see in verses 33-38. It was just outside the door that he made the great proposition that Rebekah should be the wife of Isaac, and he waited for the answer before entering the home. This corresponds exactly with Christian experience. After we are justified, the Holy Ghost in some way draws us on to entire consecration, and in a certain sense makes a proposition that we be willing to abandon ourselves without any limit to the Lord Jesus to be His and His alone forever. Upon that decision depends the future whether the Holy Spirit as the Comforter will enter into our hearts or not. In a certain sense the Holy Spirit stands just outside the door and waits for us to give our complete and final answer of leaving and going with Christ all the way, to be His alone and His forever, and the Spirit waits for our answer before He comes in with His Pentecostal endowments.

7. As soon as Rebekah agreed to leave home and friends and everything in the world and follow Eliezer to be the wife of Isaac, then the old steward entered the home and partook of the feast and rested for the night. See verses 50, 51. In the same way when the believer surveys all the points in his heart and life and deliberately dedicates himself to the blessed Jesus without any limit as to what may or may not come in his life, without any limit as to what Christ's demands may be, without any limit to his faith and devotion, it is

then that the Holy Spirit puts His seal upon such a perfect heart yielding. He enters the believer with a marvelous fulness and richness of heavenly gifts, and finds a resting place in the soul that has fully accepted Jesus as a Saviour from sin and self. It is the office of the Holy Spirit to communicate to the believer the will of God and the work of Christ. Whenever the believer reaches certain conditions of faith and obedience there will be responsive touches from the Holy Spirit which form the true sealing of the believer's faith.

8. We notice in the next step of this wonderful history that when Rebekah gave her complete decision to be the wife of Isaac, then Eliezer opened up a great store of precious things which he had brought out of the wealth of Abraham for the chosen bride. We read in verse 53 that he brought forth many gifts, rich garments, and precious things to give to the elect bride. Will you please notice the difference between these two gifts. The first at the well consisted of a ring and a bracelet; but later on in the house, after she had made public her entire devotion to Isaac, to be separated and leave all to be his wife, then the steward gave her a large dower of many rich and precious things. This corresponds exactly with the full believer in Jesus. When the child of God has entered into a boundless covenant to belong wholly to the Lord, then the Holy Spirit pours into that believer a marvelous enlightenment and a sweetness of rest and an overflow of love and a rich variety of spiritual gifts which correspond exactly with these great treasures given to Rebekah.

Furthermore, it is said that when Rebekah received these precious things that Eliezer also gave gifts to her mother and other members of the family, so that the whole family was enriched by the overflow of blessing that was given to Rebekah. This is exactly what takes place when believers receive the baptism of the Spirit. They not only get marvelous riches from God, but other Christians in the same family or the same church or the same religious association receive also great blessing as an overflow or surplus bestowed upon the believer that receives his Pentecost. What a marvelous plan God has, that there is always a surplus and overflow in His blessing, corresponding with the words of David, "My cup runneth over." You remember in the book of Leviticus that at the feast of Pentecost the people were commanded not to reap their harvests in a penurious way, but to leave some grain in the fence corners and leave the gleaning for the poor and the stranger. This indicates clearly that the feast of Pentecost meant an overflow of blessing. That fact is perfectly set forth in this lesson when Rebekah, the elect bride, not only was flooded with manifold treasures, but that her family also received many gifts as the overflow of her blessing.

9. When Eliezer wanted to leave the next morning, Rebekah's mother and brother tried to hinder the old man and requested a delay of ten days. But Eliezer was under the guidance of the Holy Spirit, and he knew that that suggestion came from the flesh, and that such a delay would hinder God's plan and might be followed by serious consequences. Hence he said, "Hinder me not," and insisted on going at once upon the long journey. This agrees with religious experience in the fact that when a full believer is filled with the Spirit and wants to go forward at once in obeying God, there will always be some fleshly minded friends or relatives that want to put a check on the fervor of the full believer. They seek in various ways to tone down the obedience and delay the steps of service, not knowing that such delays would mar God's plan and hinder the work of grace. Nothing but the light of the Holy Spirit can show the true believer, as He showed Eliezer, that our only safety is in prompt obedience, and not heeding the advice of cold and worldly friends in a matter where God's will is concerned.

10. After leaving the home of Rebekah they had a long journey, riding on the camels, and we can be sure that the burden of their conversation during that journey would be concerning Isaac. Eliezer confidently told Rebekah the whole story of Isaac's life, about the time of his birth, and then the casting out of Ishmael, and then his being offered upon Mt. Moriah, and of all the sweet and beautiful things in Isaac's life. This wonderful story of the old steward only made Rebekah love Isaac more and more and long to see him. As they moved on day after day on the swaying backs of the camels Rebekah would doubtless revolve in her mind many pictures that Eliezer gave her out of Isaac's life, until her heart glowed with a strange warmth and a wonderful attraction toward that rich land

in the west and the great and good man that she was to meet. This agrees with the fact that the true believer, after receiving the Pentecostal blessing and the gifts of the Spirit, is to go on a journey with the Holy Spirit to meet the blessed Jesus in His coming and Kingdom. As they journey together the Holy Spirit will do what Christ said, and take the things of Christ and reveal them to the soul, and thus intensify the believer's faith and love and cause him to press forward more vigorously in the path of faith and obedience.

11. At last when the journey ended we see in verse 63 that Isaac goes out to meditate in the evening time and looks up and sees the camels coming with the chosen bride in the company to meet him. When Rebekah finds out that the man she sees in the distance is her future husband, she alights from the camel and puts on her veil and prepares to meet him. What a beautiful parable this is of the winding up of the church age. When the evening time comes of this dispensation, and the sun is about to set, Jesus will come out on the blue sky, as Isaac did in the open field. The Holy Spirit, Who has been leading the chosen bride through this age, will make known to the bride the person of Jesus when He appears. And then the bride, under the guidance of the Holy Spirit, will humble herself and put on those finishing touches of preparation to meet her Lord and Husband.

12. It is said that after Isaac took Rebekah he loved her, and he was comforted over the death of his mother. How truly this fits in with the history of the blessed Jesus, for you remember how He grieved over poor old dead Israel and how He sat on Mt. Olivet and shed tears over the downfall and the doom of the old mother Israel. But after His death and resurrection He then began to gather out another company, a heavenly company. When that company shall be completed and Jesus returns to take them away to Himself unto the marriage supper of the Lamb, how true it will be that He will then be comforted in His own chosen bride, gathered from all nations and washed in His blood. There will come to His great heart a solace that will more than compensate for the death of old mother Israel in the winding up of her Jewish age.

Thus we see a series of living pictures in which Isaac is a most perfect type of the Lord Jesus, and Rebekah is a beautiful picture of the chosen ones who are to form the Bride of Christ and sit with Him in His throne and take part with Him in reigning over the nations of the earth, as we find promised in Revelation 3:21.

30

Isaac a Type of Christ

It will help us to discover the infinite magnitude and variety in the person and character of the Lord Jesus if we study and put together all the various types that are used in the Old Testament to set Him forth, and also all the various persons that were used as types of His character and life and work. There is such a fulness in Christ that it takes a great many different characters to represent Him. And when all the types have been exhausted there remains a boundless ocean of perfection and glory and virtue in Christ which can never be fully apprehended by our minds.

Among the persons in the Old Testament that are special types of Christ we may mention that Seth is a type of Christ in the one feature of being a substitute. Moses is a type of Christ as being a prophet. Joshua is a type of Christ as a warrior. Samson is a type of Christ as dying to save his people. Jonah is a type of Christ in his burial three days in the earth. Joseph is a type of Christ in relation to his brethren, the Jews. David is a type of Christ as a king. Melchizedek is a type of Christ as a priest. But Isaac is a special type of Christ as a perfectly obedient son. There is not a more perfect picture of sonship recorded in the Bible than that of Isaac.

Abraham in a spiritual sense is faith; Isaac in a spiritual sense is sonship; Jacob in a spiritual sense is service; and the twelves sons of Jacob in a spiritual sense are the twelves manner of fruit on the tree of life. Hence as Abraham begat Isaac, so faith begets sonship; as Isaac begat Jacob, so sonship begets service; and as Jacob begat the twelve patriarchs, so service produces twelve manner of fruit in the spiritual life. What I am saying is not accidental, but all these things are absolute facts in the spiritual world as truly as those men were facts in the physical world. Let us put together the points in which Isaac was a prophetic type of Christ as a son.

1. In the cases of both Isaac and Jesus their births were foretold, and their names were foretold. God said to Abraham, "Sarah shall bear thee a son, and thou shalt call his name Isaac" (Gen. 17:19). And the angel said to Mary, "Thou shalt bear a son, and thou shalt call His name Jesus." In both cases there was the supernatural element in their birth. Jesus was conceived by the Holy Ghost and born of the virgin, and Isaac had his birth from a divine quickening of the dead organs in Sarah's body. Thus he became in that sense a prophetic sample of the birth of Christ as the Son of God.

2. In both instances of Isaac and Jesus, when they were born they were the true heirs to inherit absolutely and forever all the property of their father. Isaac was the only heir that was ever mentioned in connection with Abraham. It is true that Abraham gave certain properties to Ishmael, and later on to the children of Keturah, his second wife, but they were not his heirs in the true sense of the word. In like manner the Lord Jesus is the only heir of the Eternal Father, inheriting from the Father all the possessions in the created universe by virtue of His being the only begotten Son. And then, in addition to that, He inherits everything in this world and in connection with redemption by virtue of His being born of a virgin, the second Adam. This makes Him the heir not only to the universe, but in a special sense to this world and the human race. We, as believers, become heirs of God only because we are joined on to Jesus by the new birth. And it is by virtue of our oneness with Christ that we share His inheritance, and that inheritance is exceedingly beyond all of our comprehension concerning it.

3. Isaac and Jesus were both hated by their brethren. Isaac was hated by Ishmael, and the hatred sprang out of envy and jealousy. This was exactly the case with the Lord Jesus. All the hatred that the Jews had for Christ grew out of envy and jealousy because of His infinite superiority, and because of His favor with the people, and because of the special power that the Father put upon Christ. But the hatred was especially against Him on account of His holiness.

4. Isaac and Jesus were both offered up in sacrifice, and on the same mountains, for Mt. Moriah where Isaac was laid on the altar is a part of the same mountain upon which Christ died. The special

feature connected with the offering of Isaac was that of his perfect obedience. You must remember he was about fifteen years of age when he was laid on the altar to be slain, and if he had been disobedient he could have run away from his father or resisted the binding. But there is a whole world of secret truth concerning the willingness of Isaac to die that has not been mentioned in Genesis.

I am sure that if Ishmael had been allowed to remain in the home of Abraham he would have either killed Isaac out of jealousy, or else he probably would have spoiled his faith and injected infidelity or disobedience into his mind. But because Ishmael, the carnal child, was purged out of the home it left Isaac free from contamination. He could then grow up in union with his father in a state of pure faith. Hence when the time came for him to be offered up, he had such boundless love and faith for his father's God that he was willing to die. He probably also shared his father's faith in the fact that he would have been raised from the dead, and the promise would have been fulfilled that in his seed all the nations of the earth should be blessed.

This was the one great feature in the sacrifice of Jesus, that it was made in a spirit of boundless love and faith and obedience, for the apostle mentions the fact that Christ was obedient unto death, even the death of the cross. Isaac was the first son mentioned in the Bible to be offered up in sacrifice, and there is a close union between the offering of Isaac and the offering of Jesus.

5. Just as Isaac carried upon his shoulder the very wood upon which he was to be offered up and to be burned to ashes, so Jesus carried upon His shoulder the very cross upon which He died. And thus we have a likeness between the wood that Isaac carried and the cross.

6. There is a likeness in the resurrection of Jesus and the typical resurrection of Isaac. We are told by the apostle in Hebrews 11:19 that Abraham expected God would raise Isaac out from the dead after he had been slain and burned to ashes. And then the apostle says that Abraham did receive Isaac from the dead in a figure, and that figure set forth the resurrection of Jesus from the dead. As I have said previously, this case of Isaac is the first place in all the

Bible where the resurrection is referred to, and hence it becomes in a special way a prophecy of the resurrection of Christ.

There is another point mentioned in connection with the offering up of Isaac that is too valuable to be passed over, and that is in the matter of unlimited increase and multiplication of the seed of Abraham on account of his offering up of Isaac. We read that the Lord said to Abraham, "By myself have I sworn, that because thou hast done this thing, and hast not withheld thy son, thine only son, that in blessing I will bless thee, and in multiplying I will multiply thy seed as the stars of the heavens, and as the sand which is upon the seashore; and thy seed shall possess the gate of his enemies; and in thy seed shall all the nations of the earth be blessed; because thou hast obeyed my voice" (Genesis 22:16-18).

Jesus announced the great law of reproduction when He said that if a grain of corn remained alive it never increased, but that if it was planted and died it would multiply into a great harvest. That law runs throughout all creation and all life, both in the natural and the spiritual world. If Isaac had not been offered up there would have been only one Isaac. But when his father offered him up in sacrifice and he virtually died and rose again, then out of that God decreed that there should come countless multitudes of other Isaacs that should bless all the nations of the world. Isaac was the grain of corn, and by his being planted in death there has come forth vast harvest fields of corn.

This is the fact that Jesus mentioned in connection with Himself, for if Christ had not died there would have been only one Christ. But by His death and resurrection He became the seed corn out of which should sprout and grow countless millions of Christians— that is, other Christs in a minor sense, those who are like Christ, those who have the life and character of Christ, and those who share the glory and destiny of Christ. There is a fathomless significance in dying. Hence in this respect we see a marvelous unity between the typical resurrection and multiplication of Isaac and the resurrection and multiplication of the blessed Lord Jesus.

You will also notice that when Isaac received his figurative resurrection that the "star" seed is mentioned first and the "dust" seed is mentioned last. In the original promise the "dust" seed came first and the "star" seed came next because, as Paul says, first that which is natural, and afterward that which is spiritual. But when we come into the resurrection state then things are reversed and the "star" seed come first and the "dust" seed come next. This is because when Jesus returns from Heaven with His glorified saints they will take the precedence over the living Jews who are on the earth. Hence in the millennium age the glorified saints, who are the "star" seed, will outrank the living Jews, who are the "dust" seed that will be upon the earth. We must never forget that all these words are absolutely inspired, and also the order in which the words are placed is inspired.

7. After Isaac had been offered up and restored to life again his father then sent a special agent to secure him a wife from Abraham's kindred. This was a clear prophecy that after Christ died and rose from the dead, the Father would send the Holy Ghost among God's kindred in all the earth to gather out a chosen company to form the bride of the Lamb. When Rebekah left her home to marry Isaac her brother Laban offered a prayer for her which was evidently inspired by the Holy Ghost. In a natural sense it was a great deal larger than Laban's mind, for he said to her, "Be thou the mother of thousands of millions." It is very evident that such extravagant words would not be spoken by Laban in a natural way, for thousands of millions stretch away into the countless multitudes. And this evidently was a prophetic intimation of the countless millions that are to be blessed in the ages on ages to come from the ministry of Jesus and His glorified bride.

8. We are told that later on in the life of Isaac he sowed and reaped a harvest of a hundred fold. Genesis 26:12. This is a beautiful picture that adorns the later years of that tranquil life of prayer that Isaac lived. It is a beautiful prophecy of the blessed Lord Jesus, that He is to plant and reap a hundred fold. He is to plant one grain of wheat and get one hundred grains in return, plant one life and get a hundred lives in return, and then plant those hundred lives and reap a hundred fold, and so on throughout the successive ages.

The more types we find of Christ in the Bible, the more it multiplies and enlarges Jesus to our vision. If we stand in front of a mirror we see ourselves reflected only once, but if we stand between two mirrors our image will be reflected a countless number of times. And so if we read the Scriptures only from one standpoint, that is all we see. But if we regard all Scriptures as a manifold prophecy of Christ, it is like standing between two mirrors, and we see the glorious character of our Lord reflected in an infinite degree, which makes the holy Word of God so much more valuable and beneficial to our souls.

31

Jacob at Bethel

God's Word is not only written out in His creation and His promises and prophecies, but also in the lives of His servants. The book of Genesis is filled up more with the biographical word of God than any other book in the Bible. It was appropriate that in the lives of the patriarchs God should write out the first revelations of His will in the form of human experience and providence, before the definite formation of His plan in the kingdom of Israel or in the Christian church. Bible doctrine did not produce godly living so much as the godly living of the patriarchs was the fountain out of which came Bible doctrine.

God has allowed Himself to be called the God of Jacob ten times more than He is called the God of any other man in the Bible. This is not because of Jacob's superiority to other patriarchs, but because his life in a very special way was a prophetic life of the history and destiny of the twelve tribes of Israel. And because he lived such a prophetic life is the reason why he is so frequently denominated as that one man after whom God is named. In the 27th and 28th chapters of Genesis we have the account of Jacob's leaving his father's house and going to his relatives in Padan-aram, and the first part of that journey is occupied with his experience at Bethel. If we put together the items recorded of Jacob's Bethel experience we have the following points:

1. Jacob was prompted by a double motive to leave his father's house and go to his kindred in the East. His mother, Rebekah, told him that Esau would seek to slay him and that he must flee for his safety to her brother's house in the East. On the other hand his father Isaac told him to go to his relatives and seek a wife, for he did not wish him to marry any of the ungodly women among the daughters of Canaan.

146

Here we see the double motive power under which Jacob acted. One was the motive of fear that Esau might kill him, the other was a motive of love, to seek a wife from his mother's kindred. How this illustrates the great law of life under which we all act, namely, the motive power of fear on the one hand, and of hope on the other. The motive of fear had reference to his unrighteous conduct in defrauding his brother of the heritage and was something in the past. On the other hand his motive of hope included brighter prospects for much better things in the future.

We are so constituted that we must act under the force of various motives, either of fear or of hope. The one is a propelling force and the other is an attractive force; the one drives us away from something in the past, the other drives us on to something in the future. Hence we see written out in the most vivid form in the lives of the patriarchs those great spiritual and mental laws which have controlled the actions of the human race in all generations.

2. In Jacob's dream we have a method of God's providence in communicating with His servants in all generations. You will remember that Jacob had no Bible such as we have, and no organized religious church or system of divine teaching. Hence in those early days God was laying the foundation of all religious doctrine in the lives of His servants, and He used dreams as vehicles to communicate fundamental truth to His people. In a dream a man is in the most helpless condition possible to be. While in a state of sleep his body is absolutely helpless and his mind is, in a certain sense, at sea, without rudder or compass, and in a condition detached from the outer things of the senses, so that God can deal in a most immediate and personal way with the soul. God has not ceased at any time in the world's history to communicate things to the minds of His people in dreams, and also many cases have occurred in which God speaks to the ungodly in warning in dreams. While there are a countless number of dreams that are of no significance, yet when God speaks to one of His children in a dream, it is always of such significance that the true believer can understand it and interpret it and have a personal assurance that the thing is from the Lord.

3. The ladder that Jacob saw in his dream was a special type of the Lord Jesus Christ, with its feet on the earth and its top in Heaven, setting forth in a figure the ministry of the Son of God. He stood upon this earth and at the same time by His divine nature He was in Heaven with the Father. In the first chapter of the Gospel by John Jesus refers to this fact, that He was the fulfillment of Jacob's ladder dream, when He said to Nathanael that they should see the angels of God ascending and descending upon the Son of man. The place where Jesus spoke to Nathanael was not far from the locality where Jacob had this dream. And doubtless there was something in the conversation between Jesus and Nathanael that reminded that disciple of the patriarch Jacob and his dream. Jesus is the true connecting link between Heaven and earth, and between God and mankind. He is the true ladder by which the sons of men climb up to God and into Heaven, and also the true mediator between God and man by which we have the ministry of the angels.

4. We see in this dream that God recognized Jacob as one of His real children, and embraced in the covenant that God had made with Abraham and Isaac. It is a serious perversion of Scripture to undertake to represent that Jacob at this time was a common sinner, out of saving relation to God. Jacob saw the Lord standing at the top of the ladder and he heard Him say, "I am the Lord God of Abraham thy father, and the God of Isaac." In addition to this God promised him the inheritance of the land whereon he slept, and he heard the Lord say, "I am with thee, and will keep thee in all places, and will bring thee again into this land, and I will never leave thee." These words prove most positively that Jacob at that time was a true servant and child of God, and that all subsequent blessings and covenants that God gave to Jacob were based upon the fact that Jacob was a child of God.

5. When Jacob awoke he recognized that the place where he had slept was the house of God and the gate to Heaven. Note the contrast between the house of Isaac from which Jacob had fled, and the house of God, where he now was, in the open field, with no roof above him but the blue sky. In the house of Isaac Jacob was in danger of losing his life, but in the house of God, where he had

his dream, there was ample safety and protection from Jehovah and the guardianship of the holy angels. In the house of Isaac there was ground for fear, but in the house of God there was ample assurance of hope and a bright prospect for things of the future. He said, "God is in this place and I knew it not," from which we may learn that God is always nearer to us than we are apt to comprehend.

God takes more interest in us than we take in Him. God comes closer to us than we understand, and it takes us a long while to fully grasp the intimacy of God's relation to us and to clearly apprehend His perpetual presence in our hearts and lives. And then Jacob said that that place was the gate of Heaven. They are the first words in the Bible concerning the gate of Heaven, and they form, as it were, the germ words out of which come all other references to the gate of Heaven. Jesus referred to this gate as being very difficult to enter, for He said, "Strait is the gate, and narrow is the way, which leadeth unto life."

If you will stop to study the likeness between Jacob's experience at Bethel and that of the new birth you will find food for thought and much similarity. Jesus said, "Except a man be born again, he cannot enter the kingdom of heaven." And when Jacob had his dream he found himself in the gate or the entrance way into the house of God, or the Kingdom of God. St. John tells us of the vision he had of the New Jerusalem while in Patmos, and he saw twelve gates, and upon those gates the names of the twelve sons of Jacob. There must be some connecting link that stretches across the long centuries between Jacob's dream at Bethel and the New Jerusalem which will come down from God out of Heaven in the new creation.

When Jacob spoke of being in the gate of the house of God, he certainly had reference to a spiritual house, because there was no material building over his head except the great dome of the sky. Inasmuch as the apostles refer to God building a house of redeemed souls, a great spiritual structure, which is to be formed out of redeemed human beings, it is evident that the Holy Ghost gave Jacob a spiritual insight of and an apprehension of that great house which should be formed in time to come. We must remember that God revealed the things concerning the Kingdom of Heaven and the resurrection and the city of the New Jerusalem to the patriarchs long before they were described in the New Testament. We are told that Abraham had revealed to him a city which hath foundations, and it is evident that that revelation to Abraham had been communicated to Isaac and Jacob, who were, with him, the heirs of the same promise.

The last item concerning Jacob's Bethel experience was that of the covenants which he made with the Lord. We must remember that at the time of these events Jacob had not yet reached that state of pure and unmixed faith which he entered into twenty years later. Hence his covenant was on a lower plane than that which Abraham made, and which Jacob also made many years after. When God spoke to Jacob at Bethel His words had no "if" in connection with them, as you can see by reading Genesis 28:13-15. But when Jacob made his covenant he put an "if" into it and said, "If God will be with me, then He shall be my God, and I will give Him the tenth of all I receive." Any covenant we may make with God must be measured by our faith in God and the degree in which we apprehend His person and character and relation to ourselves. And also the covenant that Jacob made was conditioned on bread to eat and raiment to put on. But that must not be understood to be of a selfish nature, but only because food and raiment are the first great essentials to our earthly life. We always put the things of our earthly life first, until we ascend into a higher knowledge of God and learn to put spiritual things first and temporal things as only secondary.

It is certain that Jacob at Bethel had an experience with God which marked an epoch in his life. From that day to this it stands forth in the Word of God as indicating that a similar epoch must come in our lives. In a state of helplessness and loneliness we must meet with God and recognize His personal dealings with us, and recognize the fact that we enter into the gate of Heaven by the new birth and come into that place in the spiritual life where we deal with God personally and enter into a covenant of fellowship with Him.

32

Jacob at Peniel

There is a space of twenty years between the Bethel and Peniel experiences of the patriarch Jacob. In Genesis 32 and 33 we have the account of the Peniel epoch in the life of Jacob. There are many contrasts between Bethel and Peniel, as, for instance, at Bethel he was going from his father's house, and at Peniel he was returning back again. At Bethel he was going toward the east; at Peniel he was going west. At Bethel he was alone and poor; at Peniel he had quite a multitude with him and was rich. At both Bethel and Peniel he met the angels of God. At Bethel he found the house of God, but at Peniel he found the face of God. At Bethel he saw God up in Heaven, at the top of the ladder, but at Peniel he saw the living Jehovah face to face and wrestled with Him as a man with a man. At Bethel Jacob slept through the night, but at Peniel he was awake all night long.

When the angel began to wrestle with Jacob he was supposed to have been a man, but as the hours passed on and the wrestling increased the man turned out to be the living Jehovah. How this sets forth the fact that God always grows on us and on the knowledge of those who study divine things. At first God comes to us and the world in humble and simple ways. But as we deal with Him in personal relationship and become acquainted with Him He grows on us, until we discover that He is the infinite and eternal God Who has made us and redeemed us. The way that the Son of God comes into the world as a little infant and then grows on the acquaintance of those who met Him, and grows in history and in the experience of the church until the evidences of His being the absolute God of the universe becomes overwhelming, is a sample of the way that God deals with the world in all things and in all generations.

The more we become acquainted with a mere man the weaker we find he is, but the more we become acquainted with God He grows on us in every direction until His power and love and attributes stretch away beyond the grasp of our understanding. Everything in human nature comes to a limit, but everything in God is forever expanding beyond all the measurement of our minds.

The wrestling of Jacob and the angel was a special divine providence, not only for the sake of Jacob, but also a sample of how God wrestles with His people throughout all generations in order to conquer them and bring them into a place of perfect subjection and docility, where they pass into the zone of the triumphant life of faith and divine union.

And then what a world of significance is in the confession that Jacob made of his name and of his nature as well. The word "Jacob" means "a supplanter," and when he confessed his name to the Jehovah angel it was a perfect unbosoming of his inner being to God, and a confessing of every secret trait of his heart to the Lord. A true confession of the heart is not only an acknowledgment of our actions, but a sincere and perfect acknowledgment of our nature, of the bottom of the heart, of the thoughts and intents of the mind, of the secret fountain of the soul out of which all actions and words proceed.

It is this boundless confession of what is in the heart that meets the conditions upon which Jesus has promised forgiveness and cleansing and the impartation of His Holy Spirit. The confession of Jacob at Peniel of his nature and his name is a sample put down in Scripture to be reproduced in the lives of countless thousands of God's people. And then you see how it was on the condition of this perfect confession that the Lord changed his name and said, "Thy name shall be no longer Jacob, but Israel, for as a prince thou hast prevailed, and hast power with God and with men."

When the Lord touched the thigh of Jacob and made him lame, that was the point where Jacob ceased to be strong in himself, and from that time onward his strength was drawn from Jehovah and not from himself. It was at that point that Jacob crossed over the zone of the old self into the region of the victorious life in the Lord his God.

There are three zones in the physical world and they have their counterpart in the three zones of the spiritual life. There is the frigid zone of being dead in trespasses and sins. Then there is the temperate zone, which is of a mixed character, partly carnal and partly spiritual. And then there is the torrid zone of perpetual summer, where the believer renounces everything of himself and enters into the warm, tender, humble love that flows from unbroken communion with the Sun of Righteousness. This condition of heart and life cannot be reached by argument or by logic or by preaching or by a slow, gradual growth or by the works of the flesh or by sacraments, or by anything known and recognized as of the human or of the flesh, but it can be reached by prevailing prayer. We never can conquer others in the true sense until God conquers us. Jacob could not prevail with Esau until after God had first prevailed with Jacob. When the Devil makes any one lame they are ruined, but when God makes us lame it is our strength and our highest achievement.

Jacob said the name of the place should be Peniel, which means "the face of God." Jesus promised His disciples that they should receive the Holy Spirit, and that the Holy Spirit would take the things of God and reveal them to the disciples. Among those things that were promised to be revealed was included a spiritual apprehension of the face of Jesus Christ. We know that this was involved in the promise because St. Paul, writing to converted Gentiles who never had seen Jesus, told them that the same God that shone out of darkness at the creation would shine into their hearts to give them the light of the knowledge of the glory of God in the face of Jesus Christ. The face of God is the highest revelation that can possibly come to a man or an angel. A vision of that face is the seal of triumphant grace, the pledge of pure love, the condition of boundless peace.

Before Jacob and the angel wrestled all night, Jacob sent a very liberal present ahead of him to appease his brother Esau. But after he got the victory from Jehovah he then put himself in front of the procession, and went forward to meet Esau with triumphant love flooding his soul. When the Lord had melted Jacob in the sweet furnace of divine manifestation, then Jacob had the power to melt his brother Esau. Peniel was to Jacob what the burning bush was to Moses, and what the day of Pentecost was to the disciples.

153

33

Joseph's Two Dreams

Of all the twelve sons of Jacob, Joseph was pre-eminent for piety and righteousness. He was above all the others a true prophet of God from his childhood, and one of the most remarkable types of Christ in the Old Testament, especially of Christ in His relation to His brethren, the Jews. We shall have occasion in the next chapter to trace out the wonderful likeness between Joseph and Jesus, but in this chapter we want to study the significance of the two dreams that Joseph had when he was probably about twelve years of age, and which are recorded in Genesis 37:5-11. Those dreams were inspired of the Holy Spirit, because they constitute a part of the infallible Word of God. They are preserved in Scripture for our benefit, as all other things that occurred in the Old Testament are for our benefit, that the man of God may be perfect and thoroughly furnished unto all good works.

"And Joseph dreamed a dream, and he told it to his brethren: and they hated him yet the more. And he said unto them, Hear, I pray you, this dream which I have dreamed: For, behold, we were binding sheaves in the field, and, lo, my sheaf arose, and also stood upright; and, behold, your sheaves stood round about, and made obeisance to my sheaf. And his brethren said to him, Shalt thou indeed reign over us? or shalt thou indeed have dominion over us? And they hated him yet the more for his dreams, and for his words. And he dreamed yet another dream, and told it his brethren, and said, Behold, I have dreamed a dream more; and, behold, the sun and the moon and the eleven stars made obeisance to me. And he told it to his father, and to his brethren: and his father rebuked him, and said unto him, What is this dream that thou hast dreamed? Shall I and thy mother and thy brethren indeed come to bow down ourselves to thee to the earth? And his brethren envied him; but his father observed the saying." In studying the points in these dreams let us consider:

1. The first dream was on the earth, in connection with reaping a field of grain, but the second dream was in Heaven, in connection with the sun, moon, and stars. In this respect the two dreams follow the pattern of everything that is written in the Scriptures. The Apostle Paul puts it down as a universal law of the unfolding of spiritual truth—first that which is natural, and afterward that which is spiritual; first that which is of the earth, and second that which is of Heaven. But while this is true, let us not forget that things which are revealed on the earth are patterns of things in the heavens, showing that the things in the heavens existed first, and the earthly things are patterned after them. And while the patterns are made known first, yet the substance of which the patterns are a copy existed first.

2. In the first dream no persons were mentioned except Joseph and his eleven brethren. The dream was confined entirely to Jacob's children, for they all were in the field reaping the grain and binding the sheaves, and the eleven sheaves of the eleven brethren did obeisance to Joseph's sheaf. In this respect the dream related in a special way to no one but Joseph's brethren.

But in the second dream there was manifested the sun, moon, and twelve stars. This included a larger number of Jacob's family, with Jacob and his wife corresponding with the sun and moon, and the twelve stars with the twelve sons. Here we see a widening in the second dream, and a truth of prophecy stretching onward into future ages and things concerning the Kingdom of Heaven with a larger significance than the first dream.

3. In the first dream we have the supply of food for the human bodies, the wheat or the grain that was reaped at the harvest. This dream had its fulfillment in later years, when, by the agency of Joseph, there was grain stored up in Egypt for the feeding of his eleven brethren and their families. And when those eleven brethren presented themselves to Joseph and bowed down to him, it was on a mission of obtaining food for them to eat. This was a perfect fulfillment of the eleven sheaves bowing down to Joseph's sheaf.

155

But in the second dream of the sun, moon, and stars there was a prophecy that Joseph should be the divinely chosen one to supply the family with light and knowledge and prophetic illumination on things to come. The dream about the wheat sheaves referred to food, but the dream about the sun, moon, and stars referred to knowledge, wisdom, and instruction, and especially the knowledge of prophecy concerning things to come in the kingdom of Israel, and later on the things concerning the Kingdom of Heaven.

Spiritual knowledge is food for the soul as truly as bread is food for the body. God not only made Joseph to be the one to supply bread for his father's family, but also to supply knowledge for their souls. Although the details are not given us in the life of Joseph, we have every reason to believe that Joseph exercised his great prophetic gift in teaching his brethren and their families a deeper knowledge of God and of things to come than they had ever learned before they went down to abide with Joseph in the land of Egypt.

David remarks in one of the Psalms that it was by Joseph that the senators of Egypt were instructed in wisdom. If Joseph gave instruction to the rulers of Egypt and their senators, I am sure he must have given a still higher degree of instruction to his father's children. We must remember that Joseph was a truly inspired prophet. Jacob recognized in the dreams of Joseph a great significance concerning things to come, for we see that while his brethren hated him because of those dreams it is said that his father "Jacob observed his sayings." The word signifies that Jacob studied Joseph's dreams and recognized in them a prophecy from God. Hence in the later years of Jacob, while he was with Joseph in Egypt, we have sufficient reason to believe that they communed together a great deal on prophetic subjects concerning their future deliverance from Egypt, and the formation of the twelve tribes into the kingdom of Israel, and the coming of the Messiah, and other kindred subjects extending on through the church age into the glorious millennium.

When Jacob received his great victorious baptism at Peniel, he told the Lord that he was "not worthy of all the mercies and all the truth that had been given to him." Have you ever noticed that he mentioned especially the truth that God had made known to him in addition to the temporal mercies? Jacob does not tell us what that truth was, but I am sure it was a vast amount of truth concerning prophetic subjects, connected with the kingdom of Israel, and the coming Messiah, and the future glorious ages beyond the resurrection from the dead.

Now this second dream that Joseph had about the stars in heaven must have had special significance in relation to the law of prophecy as well as other knowledge concerning God and the life of faith and the special mission of the twelve tribes of Israel. You see that the sheaves of wheat would be utilized in making bread and then pass away forever, but the sun, moon, and stars would go on shining throughout all future generations. This illustrates the difference between those things which are temporal and are given us only for this life, and those other things which are abiding and are to last, like faith, hope, and love, forever and ever.

4. I believe that the second dream that Joseph had has a significance in prophecy and stretches on across the long centuries into the winding up of the history of this present world, and has some relation to the vision that John saw in Patmos, recorded in Revelation 12. There have been all sorts of interpretations of that chapter in Revelation. About two-thirds of the interpretations which the various commentators have given are simply guess work, and when people guess at the meaning of Scripture, one guess is just as good as another. The only key to the Bible is the Bible itself, and I believe firmly that everything in the Bible can be explained by other things which are put in the Scriptures, and that we need not go outside the Bible to hunt for explanations of the Word of God.

Many have supposed that the woman in Revelation 12 was a type of the visible church on the earth, and that the man child was a type of the prepared saints who are caught away at the rapture, when Jesus will return. But the true spiritual church is caught away in Revelation 4:1, for chapters two and three deal with the churches of the church age, and the word "church" is not found in Revelation between chapters three and twenty-one, the new heaven and the new earth. It is true millions of sectarian church members will doubtless be left on the earth when the saints are caught away, but they do not form the true church in the Bible sense of that term. Hence there is no Bible church found on the earth during the tribulation period which begins after the close of the third chapter. This accounts for the fact that the word "church" is not used after that. We find that the nations and tongues and tribes are mentioned, and also Israel and the twelve tribes thereof, but no church.

Now it is expressly said by Isaiah that God will redeem Israel in judgment, and there is an abundance of Scripture to show that the twelve tribes of Israel are to be restored in connection with the great tribulation judgment. You will notice that chapter 12 in Revelation has all the marks connected with Israel and not the marks connected with the church. There we see the woman clothed with the sun, and the moon under her feet, and her head crowned with twelve stars. In Joseph's second dream we find reference to the sun, moon, and twelve stars. These are the only two passages in the Bible in which we find prophetic visions concerning the sun, moon, and twelve stars. It seems clear to me that both of these visions must be connected together.

When God began to work on Israel in Egypt for their deliverance, He selected at first a company of chosen holy ones to be the leaders and representatives of the Hebrew people, who took front rank in that great period of their history. Again when God began to restore the Jews from Babylon, He selected another group of eminently holy ones to be the leaders in that restoration, as Daniel, Mordecai, Ezra, Nehemiah, and other saintly prophets and priests. They became the great leaders of the restoration. In a similar way it seems to me that out from Israel, who is the mother in the time of tribulation, God will again work on His chosen people and gather out a company of eminently holy and devoted ones, at least 144,000, who will form the great leaders in connection with the last restoration of the twelve tribes.

Of course I do not speak with authority, but I simply give it out as a conviction in my mind that Joseph's dream concerning the sun, moon, and twelve stars had a prophetic significance that stretches onward throughout the Jewish age and through the church age into the tribulation period. It will be fully consummated in the millennial reign, when Israel will again be placed at the head of the nations on the earth, and they will be ruled over, as Christ says, by the twelve apostles in their glorified condition.

34

Joseph and Jesus in Humiliation

We have the life of Joseph set forth in Genesis from chapters 37 to 47, but in the first part of his life in chapters 37 to 40 we have an account of his humiliation in which there is a most perfect representation of the humiliation and the sufferings of the Lord Jesus. We have remarked in a previous chapter that Joseph is a special type of Christ in relation to His brethren, and I will call your attention to the following points where this truth is set forth.

1. Joseph was in a special way the son of Jacob's love, for he was the firstborn of Rachel, who was the wife of his special love. I have heard all sorts of remarks concerning Jacob and his two wives, and have read some things that do not agree with the Bible facts in the matter. Jacob never loved but one woman as a wife, and that was Rachel, according to the Scripture. He never bargained but for one woman, and that was Rachel. As the words are recorded in the Bible, he never mentioned but one woman by the name of wife, and that was Rachel. Leah was forced upon him by his father-in-law, and the handmaids were given to him by his wives, but there is not one single word in the whole Bible where Jacob in his heart and choice loved any woman as a wife but Rachel, or engaged for any one but Rachel.

Now Joseph was Rachel's firstborn, and hence in a pre-eminent way he was the son of Jacob's love. This beautifully illustrates what the New Testament speaks of concerning Jesus as being the Son of God's love and His dearly beloved Son. The eternal Son of God is a pure spirit the same as God the Father, and His personality was generated in the Father's bosom out of infinite love back in eternity. And so just as the Son of God is called the Son of the Father's love, so Joseph was in a pre-eminent way the son of Jacob's love.

2. Joseph was a true witness to his father concerning the conduct of his wicked brethren, and Jacob could depend with perfect assurance on the words of Joseph. So Christ is called the true witness in behalf of the Father, and a witness against sinners and against all error, and for all the truth.

3. Joseph manifested a true prophetic spirit when about twelve years old in the dreams which he had and which he published to his father and brethren. In like manner, Jesus when about twelve years of age went with Joseph and Mary to the temple and there manifested the great prophetic gift in His marvelous knowledge of Scripture, and by asking and answering questions. And just as Jacob pondered Joseph's dreams and meditated upon them, so when Jesus said, "Wist ye not that I must be about my Father's business?" it is said that Mary pondered these words in her heart, because she knew there was great significance in them.

4. Joseph was hated by his brethren because of envy and jealousy on account of his superior character and his perfect truthfulness and the consciousness of his superiority to them. In like manner Jesus was hated by His brethren, the Jews. And also He was, in His earlier years, discounted and doubted by His half brothers, the children of Mary, for it is said that His own brothers, that is, Mary's children, did not believe in Him. The basis for the hatred, both of Joseph's brethren and the brethren of Jesus, was the envy and jealousy in their hearts on account of their superiority over the other brethren.

5. Jacob sent Joseph on a ministry of kindness to hunt up his brethren and look out for their temporal welfare, and doubtless Jacob sent gifts to his other sons by the hand of Joseph. In like manner God the Father sent Jesus on a special ministry of grace to the people of Israel, for the law came by Moses, but grace and truth came by Jesus Christ. The ministry of grace always precedes the ministry of glory, and both Joseph and Jesus were ministers of grace before they became ministers of glory.

6. Joseph's brethren stripped him of his beautiful raiment which his father had given him and reduced him to great mortification and suffering. In like manner they stripped Jesus of His clothing and of that seamless robe which His friends had woven for Him. And they

161

reduced His person to contempt and humiliation before the ungodly Gentiles and all the people.

7. His brethren sold Joseph for twenty pieces of silver, which was the price of a slave boy. In like manner Judas sold Jesus for thirty pieces of silver, which was the price of a slave man. In this respect the likeness between the two is perfect. Slaves were never sold for gold, but always for silver. Hence silver is always spoken of in connection with redemption, both in the Old and New Testaments. Gold was used later on in the times of the Roman Empire, but back in the early days of the Old Testament silver was the main currency used in the buying of slaves and redeeming forfeited property.

8. They put Joseph down in an empty cistern and kept him there until they sold him to the Ishmaelites on their way to Egypt. That empty cistern was a type of the grave in which Jesus was buried. So that Joseph in one sense was buried in the earth, a prophetic type of the burial of Christ.

9. After reaching Egypt Joseph was cast into prison, a type of Hades down inside the earth, where Jesus went in spirit after His death and burial.

10. Joseph preached to two souls in prison, the chief baker and the chief butler. His preaching did not change their destiny or their character, but he simply proclaimed to each man what his destiny would be, freedom for the chief butler and death for the chief baker. This corresponds exactly with what Peter tells in his epistle, that Jesus was put to death in the flesh and quickened in the spirit, and went and preached to spirits in prison. The word "preach" that is used by Saint Peter is not the regular Greek word for preaching the Gospel, which is to evangelize. It is a term signifying a proclamation publishing certain facts to people in the disembodied state concerning His death and the destiny of those who were in the land of spirits, or in Hades.

We must remember that according to the Scriptures both in the Old and New Testaments, there were two places inside the earth called Hades, one for the righteous and one for the wicked. Jesus tells us that there was a gulf fixed between these two different localities which no one could cross over. David says in the Psalms that when God saved him He delivered his soul from the lowest hell, but it should be translated "delivered him from the lower Hades." This shows that there was a lower Hades for departed wicked souls, and an upper Hades for departed righteous souls. And that teaching in the Old Testament is confirmed by the words of Jesus in His account of the death of the rich man who went to lower Hades and of Lazarus, who went with Abraham into the upper Hades, and stayed there until the resurrection of Jesus. And then, according to Paul in Ephesians, Jesus liberated the righteous dead from the upper Hades and took them up to Paradise, somewhere in Heaven.

Joseph was put down to the very bottom of humiliation and shame in connection with his imprisonment. But in the case of our Lord and Saviour He descended infinitely lower in reproach, shame, and disgrace than Joseph descended. He went down to the very bottom of all shame and reproach, both physical and spiritual, going down to the bottom of the most disgraceful death, and then down into the regions inside the earth where departed spirits were kept.

Thus we see that both Joseph and Jesus had a perfect likeness in their lives of humiliation and suffering. Saint Paul tells us in the third of Philippians that he had a desire to share this sinking down into humiliation with Jesus, that he might by that means obtain a place in the front rank of the first resurrection.

35

Joseph and Jesus in Exaltation

In Genesis, chapters 41 to 47, we have the full account of the glorious exaltation that was given to Joseph in the land of Egypt, and this forms a picture of the exaltation of the blessed Jesus, as described in the New Testament.

1. We notice first that Joseph was lifted from the prison to the throne by an order of the king of Egypt. This is a picture of the blessed Jesus being lifted from death and having His soul lifted from Hades, and His body lifted in the resurrection by the power and command of God the Father to a place at God's right hand in the heavens. The place where the righteous dead were kept during the Old Testament dispensation was spoken of as a prison, agreeing with the prison in which Joseph was kept. Jeremiah speaks of prisoners of hope, and Peter speaks of Christ preaching to spirits in prison, so that the words all agree in significance. As Joseph was lifted from a prison, so the spirit of Jesus was lifted from prison. And the righteous dead were lifted from prison when they ascended with Christ to the upper heavens.

The apostle mentions the exaltation of Christ right in connection with His disgraceful death. He says that Christ "became obedient to death, even the death of the cross. Wherefore God hath also highly exalted Him." The reason for His exaltation was because of His obedience to a disgraceful death. This was exactly the case with Joseph, because God arranged that Joseph should be exalted because of his righteousness and his great humiliation and shame in suffering reproach while he was innocent. So in both cases the exaltation was because of the willingness of the two sufferers to undergo reproach and suffering in obedience to the will of God.

2. Joseph was speedily made the ruler of all the land of Egypt, and was seated in authority at the right hand of Pharaoh as commander

of the Egyptian nation. In like manner Jesus was exalted to the right hand of God the Father, and appointed to be the ruler over all the universe. Just as Jesus went lower down into suffering and humiliation below that of any other man that ever lived, so on the other hand He was exalted, as the apostle says, above the heavens and put higher than any other created being had ever been. He was given authority over all things, both angels and men, and over all creation, whether visible or invisible. And we are told that the only thing in the universe that was not put under the authority of Christ was the person of God the Father. Thus both Joseph and Jesus went from one extreme to the other, from unspeakable humiliation to boundless exaltation and power.

3. While Joseph was thus exalted to the throne his eleven brethren supposed him to be dead, and had no idea of his being alive in a foreign land and being honored and having such glory and power. That is exactly the case with the brethren of Jesus according to the flesh. The Jews have no conception that their Brother Jesus is really alive in a foreign country, and exalted to a throne, having dominion over all things. Just as Joseph's brethren supposed he was dead, so the Jews regard Christ as a dead man. They have no conception of His being alive and being the Lord of all things.

4. After Joseph was exalted to a throne he then obtained a wife from the Gentiles, the daughter of an Egyptian prince. In like manner, after Jesus ascended He sent down the Holy Spirit to gather out for Him a special company of believers in the Gospel age. They were to be conformed to the image of Christ, and baptized into His death and into His spirit, and rendered suitable to be a companion for Him in the ages to come. In many cases the Old Testament sets forth the doctrine of a Jewish prince marrying a Gentile wife, which was prophetic of Christ. We have samples of this in the fact that a prince of Judah married Rahab of Jericho; Boaz married Ruth, a Gentile convert from Moab; Solomon, the son of David, married the daughter of Pharaoh, the king of Egypt. And there are other passages which refer to the same subject of the Jewish bridegroom and the Gentile bride. All of these become significant in connection with our blessed Jesus and His elect church from the Gentiles.

5. In the first meeting that Joseph had with his brethren we have a prophetic type of Christ coming at the time of the rapture of the firstborn of the Church. At this time He will not be recognized by the Jews, just as Joseph was not recognized by his brethren. The conduct of Joseph in relation to his brethren is one of the most wonderful pieces of human behavior that has ever occurred in the world's history. It is of such a nature as to prove that Joseph was divinely inspired and guided in his words and in his manner. It is simply an impossibility for any man in this world to act as Joseph did, unless he was guided by the Holy Ghost. When he first met his brethren he spoke through an interpreter, and dealt roughly with them, so that it was impossible for them to imagine that the great ruler was their brother Joseph. The whole history of that first meeting will be repeated at the second coming of Christ, when He catches away the saints. At that time He will deal roughly with Israel, and speak to them through the language of strange and unexplained providences and judgments in such a way that it will be impossible for them to recognize that it is the Son of God that is dealing with them.

6. The second meeting that Joseph had with his brethren sets forth in a perfect manner the return of Christ from Heaven with His glorified saints at the close of the tribulation judgment, at which time Jesus will be revealed to all the living Jews upon the earth. You will notice that just before Joseph revealed himself to his brethren he subjected them to the climax of anguish by having them recalled and finding his cup in Benjamin's sack. All the sufferings that the brothers of Joseph had passed through reached the most acute form and terrible climax at that point in their history. They then tasted the awful anguish that Joseph felt when he was put down in the pit and sold to the Ishmaelites, and when he cried so bitterly for his brethren to spare him. God knew exactly how to adjust the judgment upon their souls, and God led Joseph in a most marvelous way to so deal with his brethren as to put them into the crucible until they felt the agony that he had felt.

Jeremiah prophesies that the Jews living on the earth will reach a climax of anguish under the antichrist in the days of the tribulation judgment. Then the race that crucified the innocent Jesus shall be made to pass through a point of anguish which to them will be like the agonies that Jesus suffered in His betrayal and death. The prophet speaks of it as the time of Jacob's trouble. Jeremiah 30.

7. When the climax of anguish had been met in the case of Joseph's brethren, he then had all strangers banished from his presence. He revealed himself to his brethren by infallible tokens so that it was impossible for them to doubt that the great ruler they were dealing with was indeed their brother Joseph. In like manner, when the Jews have met the climax of their anguish under the antichrist, and the conditions of judgment are all fulfilled, then the Lord Jesus, descending from Heaven, will reveal Himself to His own brethren, the people of Israel, by infallible tokens, "and they shall look upon me whom they have pierced, and they shall mourn for him, as one mourns for the death of his firstborn" (Zech. 12).

The words translated "they shall look upon me whom they have pierced" are very peculiar in the original and are found in no other place in the Old Testament. The word translated "me" is in the original simply the first and last letters of the Hebrew alphabet, "Aleph" and then "Tau." These words correspond with "Alpha" and "Omega" in the New Testament, the first and last letters of the Greek alphabet. They shall look on "Aleph" "Tau," that is, on "Alpha" and "Omega," which constitutes one of the names of Christ. But it is significant that that name is never used of Christ anywhere in the Bible except in connection with His second coming. Thus both Joseph and Jesus give forth to their brethren infallible proofs of their character and personality.

8. Joseph, after being reconciled to his brethren, gave them a rich portion of the country to live in, and reigned over them in perfect peace and glory the remainder of his life. Thus Jesus, after restoring Israel in the day of His return to the earth, will appoint them their heritage in the land of Canaan and at the head of the nations of the earth. He will reign over them in perfect peace and glory, in fulfillment of a great many passages of Scripture. Isaiah says that He whose name is Wonderful, Counsellor, the Prince of Peace, shall sit "upon the throne of David, and upon his kingdom, to order it, and

to establish it with judgment and with justice from henceforth even for ever" (Isaiah 9:7).

The archangel Gabriel told Mary that she should bring forth a son, and call His name Jesus, and that He should sit on the throne of His father David and reign over the house of Jacob, that is, the twelve tribes of Israel, and that His kingdom should have no end (Luke 1:32, 33). Those words must all have an exact and perfect fulfillment, which has never yet taken place, and therefore must be accomplished in the dispensation that is just ahead of us. Christ is now on His Father's throne, but He has never yet occupied His own throne, that is, His Messianic throne, which is spoken of in all Scripture as the throne of David.

Thus we see both in the humiliation and in the exaltation a most perfect correspondence between Joseph and Jesus, and the one serves to illustrate and magnify the other.

36

The Twelve Names of Israel

In the 49th chapter of Genesis we have the record of Jacob blessing his twelve sons just before his death, and uttering wonderful
prophecies concerning the destiny of his sons, especially in relation
to the latter days of their history on the earth. This record would be
wonderfully interesting simply as a history and a biography of the
twelve tribes of Israel. But when we study it as an infallible inspiration of the Holy Spirit and in relation to God's great plan concerning the kingdom of Israel, and then look forward to the outcome of
all these things in the Kingdom of Heaven, it makes this record to
swell far beyond the boundaries of natural human history, and take
on the vast significance of things as related to God in His plan for
His people throughout all the dispensations.

In a very significant way Abraham is a human type of God the
Father, and Isaac is a most wonderful type of Christ. Jacob is a very
significant type of the Holy Spirit, especially in respect to fruitful-
ness, as being the father of the twelve tribes of Israel, corresponding
to the twelve manner of fruit on the tree of life, which is the fruit
of the Spirit. Abraham, Isaac, and Jacob are earthly shadows of the
three Divine Persons in their relation to the human race, and more
particularly in relation to God's people in the different dispensations.
And when we study the significance of their lives in this respect,
it places them in their various offices in a much more interesting
light than if we simply look upon them in their order and biography.
Inasmuch as this 49th chapter gives us the names of the twelve sons
of Jacob in the natural order of their birth, we will learn much of
God's program in the destiny of Israel, and also in the program God
has made for our spiritual life and experience if we examine the significance of their names in relation to religious experience.

1. Reuben. This name signifies "Behold a son." It was the exclamation of Leah when she first saw the face of her firstborn, and the name has much significance if we look at it in the light of the new birth. The new birth is the most significant fact in our lives in relation to redemption. There is a marvelous parallel between our natural birth and our spiritual birth. Just as our natural birth is by far the most important thing that could possibly happen in our existence, so our spiritual birth is the most important thing in relation to the new creation and redemption. Just as Leah exclaimed when she saw her first infant, "Behold a son is born," so doubtless the angels exclaim when a penitent believer is regenerated, "Behold another son has been born in the Kingdom of Heaven."

2. Simeon. This name signifies "hearing," because his mother prayed earnestly for a second son, and at his birth Leah called his name Simeon because God had heard her prayer. This word "Simeon" expresses the life of prayer and answer to prayer, and shows that fact that as soon as we are born of God we are to begin a life of prayer which is to go on as long as we live. Prayer is the breathing of the heart in its relation to God, and includes every form of prayer, and is the main result of the life that we receive in the birth. And hence the name Simeon follows the name of Reuben in the same spiritual order that prayer follows the new birth.

3. Levi. This name signifies "to be joined together, to be united, as in marriage or in the most sacred bonds of mutual love and friendship." If you will read the account of the birth of all these different children you will see the reason given for the naming of each child. Leah was grieved because Jacob loved Rachel more than he loved her. She was hoping that at the birth of her third son Jacob's heart would be won over to love her, and that his heart would be united to her in supreme affection. For this reason she named her third son Levi, which means united.

It was Levi's tribe that God told Moses He would select to be the holy tribe, the priestly tribe, the tribe that in a special way stood for a perfect consecration and the perfect love of God in the heart. And hence this name represents that state of grace in the religious life of entire union with Christ, of complete devotion to Him in a life of pure love, which is produced in response to prevailing prayer. Thus we see that as Simeon, the prayer life, is the outcome of Reuben, the new birth, so Levi, or the life of divine union, is the outcome of Simeon, the life of prayer.

4. Judah. This name means "praise," and is a part of the Hebrew word "hallelujah." The word "hallelujah" means "praise Jehovah," and the name Judah is the same, only the word "Jehovah" is not all added to the name. This name of praise, thanksgiving and glorifying God is a natural result of heart holiness or divine union, which is the meaning of the name Levi. When the heart is perfectly joined to Christ it will then be a fountain of praise and thanksgiving, a true spiritual worship. Thus we see that each name has a significance which is the outgrowth of the preceding name.

5. Dan. The word "Dan" means "to judge," having the significance of judging in behalf of one that is oppressed or afflicted. Dan was the first son of Rachel's maid Bilhah. You see Rachel felt depressed in spirit because she was barren, and gave her maid to Jacob that she might bear children on her behalf. When Dan was born she exclaimed that God was now taking her part, defending her and judging on her behalf, and hence she gave him the name of Dan, or judging.

If we will follow the unfolding of the Christian life as revealed in the New Testament and in a progressive religious experience, we will find that the power to judge comes into Christian experience as a result of a life of praise and a heart of pure love. The judging power does not come at the beginning of a spiritual life, though a great many young Christians fall into the habit of judging others and of being severe in forming their opinions. But in reality the power to judge is a mature grace and requires vast charity and kindness of heart and gentleness of spirit in order to mold the opinions in such a way as to see things in the light of God.

It was prophesied by Isaiah that Jesus would not judge people according to the sight of His eyes or the hearing of His ears, but that His mind would penetrate down into the secrets of men's hearts and lives, and that He would judge His fellowmen in perfect righteousness and equity. Now it is impossible for us to exercise our faculties without in a certain sense forming opinions of people and things, and having estimates as to character. In a certain sense we must judge of others by their fruits, as Christ tells us. Now as Dan was the fifth son of Jacob, and sets forth the spiritual life in its more advanced stages, so we see that the power to judge belongs to an advanced state of grace.

6. Naphtali. This name means "my wrestlings with God." This was the second son of Rachel's maid Bilhah, and from the account given at the time of his birth we see that Rachel wrestled a great deal in prayer, that a second son might be given in her name. It was on this account that at the birth of this son she named him Naphtali, in remembrance of her earnest, agonizing prayer. This name certainly sets forth an experience in the progressive life of a true child of God, namely, an experience of agonizing prayer.

Now it is true that the word "Simeon," which means "hearing," indicates much prayer, but this name of Naphtali is a great deal stronger word. It signifies not only prayer in a general way, but a crisis of prayer, an agony of prayer, corresponding with the wrestling between Jacob and the angel. I believe that if the biography of every true Christian could be known, it would be found that in the more advanced stages of religious experience all believers have had epochs in the life of prayer in which their souls have been sorely tried. The pleading with God became so definite as to be termed a real wrestling with God, which corresponds with this name of Naphtali.

7. Gad. This word means "a troop." Gad was the first son of Leah's maid Zilpah. When Leah saw that Rachel's maid had borne two sons, then she followed the example of her sister and gave her maid Zilpah to Jacob, that she might have sons by her, but called after Leah's name. Hence when this son was born, Leah called his name Gad, because she saw, as it were, another army of sons in her name. She called the child a troop, or an army indicating that fresh reinforcements were coming to her side. This name indicates the progress of a spiritual life that a believer has to acquire as he presses on in a life of faith and under manifold testings.

8. Asher. This word signifies "happiness," and was given because this was the second son of Leah's maid Zilpah. When the boy was

born, Leah said that the people would call her blessed, or happy, and that accounts for the giving of his name Asher. It is a fact that every true believer as he advances in grace will find happiness to be a vital factor in his life. As a result of established faith and love, other people will recognize that such a believer is happy, or blessed.

9. Issachar. This name signifies "reward," and if you will read the account of his birth in a previous chapter you will notice the reason for the name. This son Issachar was born of Leah, and was her fifth son. There are various kinds and degrees of rewards, some are temporal and some are eternal, some are earthly and some are heavenly. There are certain rewards which come to the believer in this life, as where the Psalmist says concerning God's commandments, that in keeping of them there is great reward. Leah accepted the birth of Issachar as a gift from God, and hence called him "reward."

10. Zebulun. The name Zebulun signifies "dwelling, to abide, to be domesticated, to live at home in peace and quietness." Zebulun was the sixth son of Leah, and she felt so pleased that God should give her this sixth son that she felt now that she could settle down in the fullness of domestic joy and peace, and especially receive much honor from her husband and relatives. The name Zebulun indicates in the progressive life of a true believer that state of being settled, rooted, grounded in the knowledge and love of God, or that condition of being domesticated in divine fellowship and living, as it were, at home with the Lord.

11. Joseph. This word means "adding, enlargement, perpetual increase." How touching and tender are the words of God in which it is said that the Lord remembered Rachel and gave her this child Joseph, her firstborn, after so many years of weary waiting and trial. Joseph's name has the significance of the missionary. It is said that he was like a vine planted by a well of water, whose branches ran over the wall, supplying grapes not only for his own family, but also for the strangers and the Gentiles who were outside of the wall of Israel. This was most truly fulfilled in the fact that it was by him that God fed the Gentile nations with corn as well as his own family. This is surely one of the experiences that should come in the life of every true child of God, that great overflowing grace of the missionary

spirit, the enlargement of heart to love the entire human race, and to do all in our power to evangelize the nations and supply them with the Bread of Life.

12. Benjamin. Benjamin was the only son of Jacob that was born in the land of Canaan. All the other eleven sons were born in Syria, before he returned to Canaan from his sojourn with Laban. Rachel had called her son by the name of Benoni, the son of my sorrow, but Jacob changed the name to Benjamin, the son at my right hand. These two names were of great significance in the light of prophecy. When Jesus died on the cross, He was Benoni, the Son of sorrow, and especially the sorrow of Israel and for Israel; but when He rose from the dead and ascended to the right hand of God, He then became Benjamin, the Son at the Father's right hand. Benjamin was born at Bethlehem, very near the spot where Christ was born. It is the name of Benjamin, the Son at the right hand, that looks forward to the second coming of Christ. Jesus tells us that His true followers are to sit with Him in His Messianic throne when He returns to reign. And so the saints in this present state of trial are in a certain sense Benoni, but in the resurrection, when they shall sit with Christ, their name will then be Benjamin, for they shall sit with Jesus in His throne, according to His promise.

But the most significant thing that can be said of these twelve names is the fact that they are to be perpetuated in the New Jerusalem, and be engraved on the twelve gates of that city. This shows that the giving of these names was by the Holy Ghost, and not an accident. The meaning of these names is so preserved in God's plan as to extend through all the destiny of Israel in this world, and also the destiny of the Christian church, and stretch away into the oncoming ages in the new creation, and are to be preserved on the twelve gates of the golden city.

The name Benjamin is the only one of all the twelve that was given by Jacob, which is significant that those names which are given in this world, and out of human experience and human sorrow, are to be at last crowned with that name which will be pronounced in the day of rewards, "Come, ye blessed of my Father, inherit the kingdom prepared for you from the foundation of the world."

The Two Blessings of the Twelve Tribes

In closing our studies on the book of Genesis to find out God's first words bearing on the various subjects of the Bible, let us study the blessing that the patriarch Jacob pronounced upon his twelve sons in relation to the things that would take place with their posterity in the last days. These are the first words of a prophetic character in dealing with the final history of the twelve tribes. And then let us connect with Jacob's blessing that other blessing pronounced by Moses upon the twelve tribes just before his death.

I have been profoundly impressed with these two sets of blessings pronounced upon Israel by Jacob and by Moses. These two blessings supply the key to unlock the entire history of Israel both in this world and in the world to come. Israel is the key that God has made to unlock all history. After we have entered the glorified state and look back upon human history, we will be able to read the record of God's dealings with all the nations in God's light. And then we will see the meaning of all God's providences with the different nations of the earth, and be able to discern the significance of all things in human history having the destiny of Israel for the key.

Moses said: "When the Most High divided to the nations their inheritance, when He separated the sons of Adam, He set the bounds of the people according to the number of the children of Israel. For the Lord's portion is His people; Jacob is the lot of His inheritance" (Deut. 32:8). Here is an inspired declaration that God deals with all the nations of the earth in some mysterious way as they are related to the twelve tribes of Israel.

The blessing that Jacob pronounced on his twelve sons, as recorded in Genesis 49, was in the land of Egypt, just before the Hebrews passed into a state of bondage under the Egyptians, in which they served four hundred years. On the other hand the blessing pronounced by Moses upon the twelve tribes, as recorded in Deuteronomy 33, took place in the land of Moab, just east of Jericho, a short time before the death of Moses, and just before the Hebrews entered upon their history under the judges, which lasted four hundred years. The one blessing was just before their entrance into slavery, and the other blessing was just before their entrance into Canaan as an independent and free nation.

In the next place we see that Jacob blessed his twelve sons in the natural order of their birth, beginning with Reuben and ending with Benjamin. On the other hand when Moses pronounced his blessing, he changed the natural order of their names and blessed them according to a higher spiritual order which the Holy Ghost selected, in which the spiritual order takes the precedence over the natural order.

And again, when Jacob blessed his twelve sons he prophesied their future destinies according to their history in this world and in human life, extending down to the time of the great tribulation. On the other hand when Moses pronounced his blessing he opened up a prophetic destiny of the various tribes in the heavenly light of the kingdom age, when Israel shall be restored to everlasting blessing and be the head of the various nations on the earth.

In the next place, when Jacob pronounced his blessing on his twelve sons he mingled curses with the blessings, and referred to many sad and sorrowful things that would take place in the destiny of his children. But on the other hand, when Moses pronounced his blessing, there was no mention of any curse or any defeat or any failure, but every word sets forth only that which is blessed and heavenly and successful in their career.

It is enough to thrill any devout student who has a beauty-haunted mind to trace these two lines of prophecy, one from the standpoint of Egypt, and the other from the standpoint of Moab; one in the human and the other in the divine; one on the plane of human life, with its failures and sorrows, and the other on the plane of the heavenly life, with its glorious victories and successes.

These two blessings set forth an example of what the Apostle Paul refers to when he says that God gives us first that which is natural, and afterwards that which is spiritual, and that He doeth away the first in order that He may establish the second. I have searched out one hundred things in the Bible in which there is reference to two things, and in every case the second thing proves to be the uppermost and the best and the most significant, as the first and second Adam, the first and second birth, the first and second bird sent from the ark, the first and second effort of Moses to deliver the Hebrews, the first and second writing of the law on tables of stone, the first and second crossing of the Red Sea and the Jordan, the first and second veils in the tabernacle, the first and second rainbow at the flood and at the second coming of Christ, and scores of other instances. But in every single instance the emphasis is on the second thing, which is always superior in blessing. And these two blessings pronounced on the twelve tribes by Jacob and Moses correspond with all the other cases of a similar character, which manifest to us the mind of God and the character of His dealings with His people.

In a previous chapter I have given the significance of the names of Jacob's twelve children, in which we see the unfolding of the steps of a life of faith from the new birth to our being seated with Christ at His right hand in His heavenly Kingdom. Now let us study a little the twelve blessings that Moses pronounced on the tribes of Israel as he presents them, not in the natural order of the birth of those sons, but according to a higher spiritual order, which sets forth the higher destiny in the kingdom age.

1. The blessing upon Reuben was the gift of life. "Let Reuben live, and not die." Life is always the fundamental blessing, and must of necessity come first in all God's dealings with His people. God cannot bless that which is dead, and hence the gift of life is the basis of all other blessing. There are seven promises to the seven churches in Revelation, but the first is the promise of life, to eat of the tree of life, for this is always fundamental.

2. The blessing upon Judah is that God will hear his voice and answer his prayer. "Hear, Lord, the voice of Judah." Jacob put the name of Simeon next to Reuben, and the word "Simeon" also has reference to prayer, for it signifies that God heard his mother's request. But Moses puts Judah next to Reuben, although he was the

fourth son, because Judah prevailed in prayer, that God would let the Messiah be born of his line. One of the most remarkable cases of prevailing prayer mentioned in the Bible is found in 1 Chronicles 5:1, 2. Here we are told that Judah prevailed above his brethren, and on that account the Chief Ruler, that is Christ, was born of his line.

We see in the passage referred to that Reuben was the firstborn of Jacob, and he was entitled to both the genealogy and the birthright. Christ therefore should have been of Reuben's line and also Reuben should have had the birthright, that is, the property and the first rank in honor. But it is mentioned there that because he defiled his father's bed he lost both the genealogy and the birthright. Now when Reuben lost his inheritance, the next son that came in order was Joseph, because he was the firstborn of Rachel, the second wife. Joseph would have inherited both the genealogy of the Messiah and also the birthright, but only see what a miracle was wrought in answer to the prayer of Judah. Judah set himself to pray that the Messiah might come of his line. He prevailed over all the prayers of his other brethren, and also prevailed over the natural law of inheritance. God answered his prayer by causing Christ to be born of Judah's line, and this made Judah the royal son of the royal line. I regard this as one of the most marvelous things in all the Bible in relation to prevailing prayer.

We see in the passage that Joseph retained the birthright, which included the largest legacy of property and other privileges. But the genealogy, the line of blood royalty, descended from Judah, and the virgin Mary was a direct descendant of Judah, and also Joseph, the husband of Mary, was a descendant of Judah. Hence Moses, in pronouncing his blessing, refers to this subject of Judah prevailing in prayer and becoming the line out of which should be born the Chief Ruler, that is Christ. Moses pronounces his blessing according to the heavenly order, and not as Jacob did, according to the earthly order, and for this reason the name of Judah comes next to Reuben.

3. The blessing upon Levi was the grace of holiness. "Let thy Thummim and thy Urim be with thy holy one, even Levi." The word "Thummim" means "perfection," especially perfection in love; and the word "Urim" means "light, divine illumination." Levi was

chosen to be the priestly tribe and to teach the other tribes the law, and to put incense and offer sacrifices for the people, and to pray for the people and be the leader in worship and in things pertaining to holiness.

4. The blessing of Benjamin was that of the keeping power, security, safety. "Of Benjamin he said, The beloved of the Lord shall dwell in safety by him, and he shall dwell between the Lord's shoulders." The blessing of preservation follows as a natural consequence of the grace of holiness and spiritual worship and a life of constant power, and this is why the blessing of Benjamin is placed by Moses right in succession to the blessing of Levi, or the life of intercession and worship. In the natural order Benjamin comes last from the standpoint of history, but in the spiritual order he comes fourth, because his blessing in the heavenly places is that of preservation. In marching on a long journey it is the youngest child that is taken up and carried by the strong father, and the Oriental parents carry their children on their backs between their shoulders. Thus Moses represents the youngest child as being lifted in the great journey and carried between God's shoulders, the place of security and rest.

5. The blessing of Joseph is that of the fullness and overflow of all blessing, both earthly and heavenly. The word "precious," or a synonym of the word "precious," occurs seven times in the blessing pronounced on Joseph. The precious things of Heaven, and the precious fruits brought forth by the sun, and the precious things brought forth by the moon, and the chief of the precious things of the mountains, and the precious things of the hills, and the precious things of the earth, and the good will or the precious will of Him that dwelt in the bush, all these seven-fold precious things are to come down upon the head of him that was separated from his brethren.

Joseph gets the largest of all the blessings because he had the birthright which was forfeited by Reuben, and also because his two sons were adopted by Jacob as Jacob's own sons, and Ephraim and Manassah took rank with the other sons. Hence the Lord searched through all the earth and all the sky and the sun and the moon and all creation to extract every possible blessing for Joseph. And the reason was because he was separated from his brethren and was a type of Christ leaving the Jews in their dead state and going to the Gentiles and providing food for the world. It was Ephraim that led in the revolt of the ten tribes, and the tribe of Ephraim was the one that pushed the ten tribes out of Canaan and they were scattered among all nations to the ends of the earth, which fact is mentioned by Moses in his prophecy.

6. The blessing of Zebulun is that of a missionary. "Of Zebulun he said, Rejoice, Zebulun, in thy going out." This evidently is a prophecy of missionary work in the history of the spiritual life, and it will have a special fulfillment, doubtless, in the coming age in reference to Israel.

7. The blessing of Issachar is that of the domestic life. "Let Issachar be blest in their tents." I am perfectly convinced that the Koreans are the descendents of the tribe of Issachar, for I find that every word pronounced upon Issachar by both Jacob and Moses are perfectly true of that nation. The Koreans bear the heaviest burdens on their backs of any other nation of the earth, which is referred to by Jacob in Genesis 49:14.

In the next place, the Koreans are, as a rule, the most indolent people on the face of the earth and they never do any work except of necessity. Jacob said that Issachar loved to rest. And if you go to Korea you will often find three or four men at work and fifteen or twenty other men lying down on the ground and watching them, as I have seen several times when I was there. The Koreans have paid tribute for over two thousand years to either China on the west or Japan on the east. And Jacob said that Issachar should be a servant to pay tribute, which is more true of the Koreans than of any other nation that has ever lived. The Koreans are a hermit people and they never migrate like other nations. This agrees with the words of Moses that Issachar would be a people that would live at home, or in their tents.

If we apply this to the spiritual life it signifies that the true believer is to be domesticated with the Lord Jesus in a life of faith and fellowship.

8. The blessing of Gad is that of great enlargement. "And of Gad he said, Blessed be he that enlargeth Gad." All the words used by Moses concerning Gad refer to enlargement, of the getting possession of the choicest things that were possible to be had. This has its fulfillment in the progress of the spiritual life when the believer seeks in every way to extend his usefulness and service by prayer, or ministry, or philanthropy, and in every way extending the kingdom of God, and also his own usefulness and happiness. The Apostle Paul refers to this stage in the Christian life when he said to one of the churches that he had planted that if they wanted to reward him they were "to be enlarged," and their enlargement would be his recompense. Narrowness of heart and mind is always an affliction, but in the spiritual life it is more than an affliction and amounts in a certain sense to a curse.

9. The blessing of Dan is that of power, energy, victory. "Of Dan he said, Dan is a lion's whelp; he shall leap from Bashan." All the pictures that are drawn in the Bible of the spiritual life set forth a constant increase of vitality and energy down to the end. And the apostle says that while the outer man shall perish, the inward man, the spirit man, is to be renewed in strength daily.

10. The blessing of Naphtali is that of being satisfied with the favor of God. "Of Naphtali he said, Thou art satisfied with favor and full with the blessing of the Lord, possessing the west and the south" (that is, the warm side of the mountain, and where the daylight lingers longest). There is a charming picture of union, repose, and contentment in the things of God. This stage of grace is God's plan for all His servants as they pass on through the journey of a full religious experience.

11. The blessing of Asher is that of many children. "Let Asher be blessed with children, let him be acceptable to his brethren, and dip his foot in oil." In these words we notice that the spiritual life is to increase and multiply down to the very end and be fat and flourishing in old age.

In this list we notice that the name of Simeon is left out, because Moses put in the two sons of Joseph, Ephraim and Manassah, and so Simeon is omitted from the list.

We have another list of the names of the twelve patriarchs in the book of Revelation in connection with the great work when God begins their final restoration in the great tribulation. In that list the name of Dan is left out to make room for the two sons of Joseph. In the list of names given by Jacob that of Judah comes fourth, but in the list of names given by Moses the name of Judah comes second, and in the list given in Revelation the name of Judah comes first. All of this is significant concerning things that are to come. The royal tribe forges its way to the front, and comes out at last at the head of the great column of God's chosen ones in the days when the Kingdom shall come.

I have only searched out a few of the marvelous wonders of this book. There are countless other wonders which remain to be searched out, and what we do not find in this present short pilgrimage life will be found out in the ages that are to come, for I believe it is God's plan that His people shall some day come to understand every atom of His inspired Word.

The book of Genesis begins with a marriage and the last words are "a coffin in Egypt." What a panorama of human history, and what a world of great spiritual facts are revealed in this book in reference to God's dealings with the sons of men.

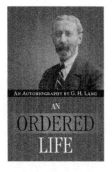

Lord, Teach Us to Pray
By Alexander Whyte

D r. Alexander Whyte (1836-1921) was widely ac-knowledged to be the greatest Scottish preacher of his day. He was a mighty pulpit orator who thundered against sin, awakening the consciences of his hearers, and then gently leading them to the Savior. He was also a great teacher, who would teach a class of around 500 young men after Sunday night service, instructing them in the way of the Lord more perfectly.

In the later part of Dr. Whyte's ministry, one of his pet topics was prayer. Luke 11:1 was a favorite text and was often used in conjunction with another text as the basis for his sermons on this subject. The sermons printed here represent only a few of the many delivered. But each one is deeply instructive, powerful and convicting.

Nobody else could have preached these sermons; after much reading and re-reading of them that remains the most vivid impression. There can be few more strongly personal documents in the whole literature of the pulpit. . . . When all is said, there is something here that defies analysis— something titanic, something colossal, which makes ordinary preaching seem to lie a long way below such heights as gave the vision in these words, such forces as shaped their appeal. We are driven back on the mystery of a great soul, dealt with in God's secret ways and given more than the ordinary measure of endowment and grace. His hearers have often wondered at his sustained intensity; as Dr. Joseph Parker once wrote of him: "many would have announced the chaining of Satan for a thousand years with less expenditure of vital force" than Dr. Whyte gave to the mere announcing of a hymn. —*From the Preface*

Buy online at our website: **www.KingsleyPress.com**
Also available as an eBook for Kindle, Nook and iBooks.

A Present Help
By Marie Monsen

Does your faith in the God of the impossible need reviving? Do you think that stories of walls of fire and hosts of guardian angels protecting God's children are only for Bible times? Then you should read the amazing accounts in this book of how God and His unseen armies protected and guided Marie Monsen, a Norwegian missionary to China, as she traveled through bandit-ridden territory spreading the Gospel of Jesus Christ and standing on the promises of God. 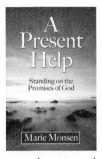 You will be amazed as she tells of an invading army of looters who ravaged a whole city, yet were not allowed to come near her mission compound because of angels standing sentry over it. Your heart will thrill as she tells of being held captive on a ship for twenty-three days by pirates whom God did not allow to harm her, but instead were compelled to listen to her message of a loving Savior who died for their sin. As you read the many stories in this small volume your faith will be strengthened by the realization that our God is a living God who can still bring protection and peace in the midst of the storms of distress, confusion and terror—a very present help in trouble.

Buy online at our website: **www.KingsleyPress.com**
Also available as an eBook for Kindle, Nook and iBooks.

THE AWAKENING
By Marie Monsen

REVIVAL! It was a long time coming. For twenty long years Marie Monsen prayed for revival in China. She had heard reports of how God's Spirit was being poured out in abundance in other countries, particularly in nearby Korea; so she began praying for funds to be able to travel there in order to bring back some of the glowing coals to her own mission field. But that was not God's way. The still, small voice of God seemed to whisper, "What is happening in Korea can happen in China if you will pay the price in prayer." Marie Monsen took up the challenge and gave her solemn promise: "Then I will pray until I receive."

The Awakening is Miss Monsen's own vivid account of the revival that came in answer to prayer. Leslie Lyall calls her the "pioneer" of the revival movement—the handmaiden upon whom the Spirit was first poured out. He writes: "Her surgical skill in exposing the sins hidden within the Church and lurking behind the smiling exterior of many a trusted Christian—even many a trusted Christian leader—and her quiet insistence on a clear-cut experience of the new birth set the pattern for others to follow."

The emphasis in these pages is on the place given to prayer both before and during the revival, as well as on the necessity of self-emptying, confession, and repentance in order to make way for the infilling of the Spirit.

One of the best ways to stir ourselves up to pray for revival in our own generation is to read the accounts of past awakenings, such as those found in the pages of this book. Surely God is looking for those in every generation who will solemnly take up the challenge and say, with Marie Monsen, "I will pray until I receive."

Buy online at our website: **www.KingsleyPress.com**
Also available as an eBook for Kindle, Nook and iBooks.

Printed in Great Britain
by Amazon